Get That Novel Written!

Get That Novel Written!

DONNA LEVIN

WRITER'S DIGEST BOOKS
CINCINNATI, OHIO

ABOUT THE AUTHOR

Donna Levin is the author of *Get That Novel Started!*, (Writer's Digest Books, 1992). She is also the author of two novels: *Extraordinary Means* (Arbor House, 1987) and *California Street* (Simon & Schuster, 1990), both of which have been optioned for film. She teaches writing at the University of California Extension at Berkeley and is a regular instructor at the Writer's Connection. She is a frequent speaker at writer's conferences and at writer's group meetings in the San Francisco area. Her book reviews air on KSFO-AM radio in San Francisco, where she also writes a monthly column called "City Mom" for the *San Francisco Independent*. She lives in San Francisco.

Get That Novel Written! Copyright © 1996 by Donna Levin. Printed and bound in the United States of America. All rights reserved. No part of this book may be reproduced in any form or by any electronic or mechanical means including information storage and retrieval systems without permission in writing from the publisher, except by a reviewer, who may quote brief passages in a review. Published by Writer's Digest Books, an imprint of F&W Publications, Inc., 1507 Dana Avenue, Cincinnati, Ohio 45207. (800) 289-0963. First edition.

This hardcover edition of *Get That Novel Written!* features a "self-jacket" that eliminates the need for a separate dust jacket. It provides sturdy protection for your book while it saves paper, trees and energy.

Other fine Writer's Digest Books are available from your local bookstore or direct from the publisher.

00 99 98 97 96   5 4 3 2 1

Library of Congress Cataloging-in-Publication Data

Levin, Donna.
    Get that novel written! / Donna Levin.—1st ed.
        p.   cm.
    Includes bibliographical references and index.
    ISBN 0-89879-696-2 (alk. paper)
    1. Fiction—Authorship. I. Title.
PN3355.L395   1996
808.3—dc20

96-11139
CIP

Edited by Jack Heffron and Roseann Biederman
Designed by Angela Lennert Wilcox
Author photo (this page) by Cherie Dyer

To Christine Mary McDonagh,

who combines the best of

Mary Poppins and Anne Sullivan.

My children will always be hers, too.

ACKNOWLEDGMENTS

Like most writers, I can't begin to acknowledge all
the people who deserve credit. These are a few:

Liz McDonough, at the University of California
Extension, who's provided me with the opportunity
to teach many committed novelists. Everyone should
have such a helpful, patient and intelligent boss.

The students who taught me much
of what's in these pages.

Jim Frey, who got me my first real teaching gig.

Adair Lara, writing partner and friend.

Abbot Bronstein, for reasons he knows best.

Bill Brohaugh, Jack Heffron and Roseann Biederman at
Writer's Digest Books, who made this book possible.

My children, William and Sonia, who also made this book
possible by letting me go up to the attic to work.

Jill Manus, the best literary agent in the world.

And last for emphasis: Michael Bernick,
mensch among *menschen*.

As good almost kill a man as kill a good book:

who kills a man kills a reasonable creature, God's image,

but he who destroys a good book kills reason itself,

kills the image of God, as it wre, in the eye.

—John Milton

It's easy, after all, not to be a writer.

Most people aren't writers,

and very little harm comes to them.

—Julian Barnes

CHAPTER ONE

Why We Must Study Craft in This Imperfect World

The Novel: Product of Genius or Hard Work? (You Be the Judge.)

When I was starting out as a writer, it seemed as though teachers were always telling me, "You have to find your voice," or "You have to just keep plugging."

Which was true enough, but not much help.

We all know that it's impossible to distill the magic of novels into a few simple rules. But we have to start somewhere. If we regard novels solely as the product of genius, then very few of us can hope to write anything of value, or even to improve upon what we can write today.

Wanting to be a writer is much the same as wanting to be a plumber. Although you must begin with native ability, you must also acquire the skills. No one is born with a plunger in her hand yelling, "Show me the clog!" No one is born *knowing* the difference between a metaphor and a simile.

Writing means living in a state of tension between surrendering to unconscious processes (something like waiting for the Muse to inspire you), and imposing a very conscious form on what you do. If you only have technique, your work will be soulless, but if you only have instinct, your work may be sloppy and too personal. (I once had a student who defended his work by saying, "It came from my unconscious, so it must belong there." Dreams come from your unconscious, too, but I wouldn't suggest that you try to publish them.)

No writing book can substitute for God-given talent. More importantly, no writing book can substitute for long, long hours of writing itself. However, by analyzing the work of others we can start to see our own work more objectively. We can learn techniques that can lead us out of plot problems, that can help us translate our emotional message into dramatic scenes, that can make our characters seem more real.

Writing is one of the more isolated callings one can pursue, but we don't work completely alone. We're links in a chain of novelists before, during and after us. "Rules" are really just statements about what has worked before. As we apply those rules to our own writing, the real magic begins: We make up rules of our own, and build on what others have done in the past.

Rita Mae Brown said, "The novel is a work of a single, unified consciousness." As such, it will always be unique. Reading books about writing or taking writing classes will not make you write like other people, will not iron out the creases in your personality. But you can look upon all the techniques we'll discuss as tools with which to construct your novel. Pick up one, give it a try; discard it if it doesn't work, maybe try it another time. Maybe you'll find a slightly different way of using it that suits you better.

In this book, I'm not going to tell how to write a novel during your coffee break, or how to make money in your sleep. What I am going to do is tell you what a lot of people, and I myself, have observed about what works, what doesn't, and why.

Writing a novel involves much trial and error and at least a little bit of luck. I also have a number of ideas about how to go about this trial and error. It's not cheating; I prefer to think of it as being efficient.

The rules provide a starting place. The journey is yours.

The Format of This Book and How to Use It

Much of the material in this book cohered for me because of the teaching I've done for over ten years now. I've worked with literally hundreds of novels in progress, and what continually fascinates me is just how passionate and talented the authors are, and how diverse their experiences and subjects are. It's been a privilege to be part of these students' and colleagues' writing careers.

This book is intended to be a comprehensive guide to novel writing. As a writing teacher, I have seen a need to define some basic concepts, such as scene breaks, point of view, chapters and even titles and epigraphs. I've found that many intelligent, well-read students are unfamiliar with how a novel is put together, because they don't teach you to be a writer in freshman English—they teach you to be a reader, by concentrating on symbolism and foreshadowing and theme (which you need to know, too). If some of the definitions here are too basic for you, consider them a review.

You will notice that the chapters are divided into two parts: *The Basics* and *The Finer Points*. If you are just starting out, you might want to go through the book reading just *The Basics* first and then perhaps come back in a month or two to read the second half.

Each chapter also has a special section on *Rewriting Notes*. You can read that now, but if you start to feel overwhelmed, save that section for completion of your first draft. But don't forget to check out the end of each chapter, most of which contain additional exercises.

A writing book requires many examples and I've tried to use a wide range. Some are invented, and some are adapted from student manuscripts. Many examples come from literature—contemporary and classic, literary and popular. More occasionally, I use plays, movies and television shows when they illustrate the principle in question. I've discovered in my teaching that it's difficult to find books that everyone has read, even among groups of well-read people. Like it or not, though, almost everyone knows the characters from *M*A*S*H* and *Star Wars*.

A while back, I wrote a book called *Get That Novel Started!* that was primarily about just what the title says: overcoming emotional barriers, organizing time and material and getting started. This book can be read as its follow-up or independently. I didn't want to have any overlap between the two books, so any aspects of craft I covered in the first book will not be covered here, with very small exceptions, when they are necessary for the sake of clarity.

Why Bother Anyway?

A long time ago, people sat around fires, or in the kitchen shelling peas, and told stories of princesses in disguise and angry gods. Telling stories is a human need: they teach and heal us. Stories connect us to each other and to our past, and in time we give them to our children. The good stories last a long time, sometimes forever. *Romeo and Juliet, Cinderella* and *Oedipus Rex* are just stories, after all, but they are also integral parts of Western culture, defining how we think about ourselves, and what we believe is right and wrong.

We always need more stories, peopled with characters we can care about, to say for us what we can't otherwise express. Write some and be immortal. I hope this book will help.

CHAPTER TWO

Character Is Destiny

THE BASICS

The Importance of Character

There's an old saying, "character is destiny." Meaning that the person you are will determine what your life is like.

Now, I'm not willing to go so far as the est graduates of the 1970s who said that people starving in developing nations had created their own hunger and had to take responsibility for it. Seems to me that things happen that we have no control over, and no one knows for sure why.

But it's fairly easy to see how, up to a point, the principle does work. A hard-working student usually gets better grades than the one who's out drinking beer with his pals every night. A thief often ends up in jail. And if you're paranoid, eventually people *do* start talking about you.

The effect of personality on our lives is further emphasized by how entrenched those personalities are. In spite of the claims of various human potential movements, it's very difficult to alter our own characters. People spend years at it with a variety of therapies, from psychoanalysis to behaviorism, and consider even very slight changes to be raging successes.

Fortunately, as a novelist, you don't have to change yourself or the world. But what you do have to do is hard enough: Become an astute observer of human nature and then find ways to translate your observations into fictional people who manage to capture all the wonder and complexity, contradiction and tenacity of the human soul.

In *The Art and Craft of Novel Writing*, Oakley Hall observed, "It is not sufficient to assemble a character by adding characteristics as grilles and fenders might be added on an assembly line: a big nose, duck-like walk, houndstooth check jacket, taste for Beethoven and the Red Sox, and a foolish fidelity to a faithless wife. The character must be produced on the page, whole and alive, his breath congealing on the air."

To produce a character "whole and alive," you must be a psychologist, parent, sociologist and friend.

And then, just as real people shape their lives, so will your fictional characters shape their plots. Thus we can take the aphorism one step further and say, "Character is the destiny of a novel." Plot is important—damn important—especially in terms of marketing your book. And as we'll see, it's only through action and conflict that we can really get to know who the characters are.

But that's what we really want to do in the end: Get to know the characters. That's what it's all about. People.

They Are What They Do: How Characters Reveal Themselves in Action

The oldest writing dictum around is, "Show, don't tell."

In terms of characterization what that means is that instead of telling us what the characters are like ("He was mean"), you should let them reveal themselves to us by their actions ("He kicked his dog every morning").

Two examples will further illustrate this in simplified form. Compare:

> She was an adorable little girl whom everyone loved, especially for the kindness she always showed to her brother.

To:

> Billy was crying. Anna lay her head on his back. "Don't cry, Billy. You can have my ice cream. I wasn't going to finish it anyway."

Who wouldn't love a kid like that? You don't need to tell us; you've shown us.

It's hard to write an entire novel without doing a tiny bit of telling. Maybe a character will sum up another for us in dialogue ("I think she's selfish") or the author herself will give us some quick information that she doesn't have time to dramatize.

But as much as possible you want to show, not tell, us because that is the way the reader can experience the character for himself.

Show who a character is by their actions.

Being told is like hearing about someone; being shown is like meeting someone.

When you show, the reader knows what the author knows but is free to draw his own conclusions about the meaning of the characters' actions. Maybe the reader really hates dogs and doesn't mind seeing them get a kick once in a while. The reader is free to root for the guy who kicks his dog, without the author getting in the way.

This creates depth in characters; it's how characters are "produced on the page, whole and alive," because you allow the characters the ambiguity and richness of real people, rather than simply pronouncing your judgment of them, or listing their characteristics.

As you write your novel, you will constantly look for opportunities to let the characters show us who they are. Often, and importantly, these will be in broad gestures that move the plot forward. Scarlett O'Hara lies to Frank Kennedy so that he'll marry her and pay the taxes on Tara; Sydney Carton takes Charles Darnay's place at the guillotine. Says a lot about both of them.

But all of your characters, from your hero and heroine down to the mail carrier who appears once, can reveal themselves constantly through their actions, great and small.

The Many Types of Actions

Characters reveal themselves in action but action itself can be broadly defined.

How We Live Our Lives—The Action of Choice

We choose what to do with our lives on a daily basis, and we choose how to respond to unusual circumstances. These choices make the most immediate, incontrovertible statements about who we are.

Jay Gatsby pursues Daisy for years, hoping to win her back. Hester Prynne refuses to reveal the identity of the father of her illegitimate child.

For most people, work occupies a large amount of their lives. What job or profession has your character chosen to pursue? The thought of a man who becomes a firefighter or forest ranger immediately brings to mind different associations than the man who chooses to become an accountant. A woman who becomes a trial attorney is different from a woman who becomes a teacher of deaf children.

How does your character face a physical, emotional or financial crisis? When the stock market crashes, does he jump from the window of his forty-fourth floor office, or does he think of a plan to help his elderly clients whose savings have been wiped out? When a woman's husband leaves her, does she go gunning for him with a rifle or does she make sure he takes a sweater?

These choices, and the resultant lifestyles, are your broadest strokes in characterization. But the many other ways in which a character might reveal herself are the smaller-tipped brushes with which you can paint in their finer lines.

Dialogue—The Action of Speaking

"Hey, Maw, pass me over some of them grits, will ya?"

"There are several provisos, to be sure, and at least one caveat . . ."

"Let go of that dame before I slug ya."

"She's all, 'he's like totally, totally rad!' And I'm all, 'Wait, he's like my dude. . . .' "

All techniques of showing bring the character to life in front of us, but dialogue is the single most immediate: We hear the character talking to us directly. The author completely disappears.

And as soon as a character opens his mouth, he reveals much about his level of education, the place he grew up, his sense of humor or seriousness, even his self-image.

And personality. Is a character taciturn or loquacious? Is she the type of woman who, when confronted with a friend's bad dye job, will hesitantly suggest, "I'm not sure you have the skin tone to be a blonde," or will she say, "Honey, you look like Madonna on a bad day"?

People use and misuse big words like "obsequious" and "etiology." They overuse obscenities. Both say something about who they are.

Verbal tics are common, and they reveal character, too. Repeated use of "Uh," "you know" or "I mean," may indicate a person is uncertain or hesitant. In George Eliot's *Middlemarch*, Sir James Chettam irritates Dorothea Brooke because he constantly says "Exactly," even when she has just disagreed with him. In Sir James this verbal tic reveals a character so bland and complacent that he doesn't even realize that he's being contradicted; nor would he care if he did realize it, because his opinions are so weakly held.

Don't forget that sometimes what's left *unsaid* can reveal character as well, as often brilliantly demonstrated by Joan Didion in her definitive Hollywood novel, *Play It as It Lays*.

The central figure of *Play It as It Lays* is Maria Wyeth, a former starlet, depressed over a recent abortion and the general meaninglessness of life, as epitomized by her fast-lane acquaintances: people so shallow that a walk through the ocean of their souls wouldn't get your feet wet. This passage is a phone conversation between Maria and a powerful Hollywood lawyer with dubious connections.

> "You were going to come over and use the sauna," Larry Kulik said.
> "I've been —"
> "So I hear."
> "Hear what."
> "Hear you're ready for a nuthouse, you want to know."
> "You think I need a sauna."
> "I think you need something."
> Maria said nothing.
> "I'm a good friend to people I like," Larry Kulik said. "Think it over."

Larry Kulik is coming on to Maria, offering to advance her career in exchange for sexual favors. Not only does Didion convey this through what's left unsaid, but she conveys both characters' cynicism, despair and ennui. (Unfortunately, creating such subtext is harder than it looks, as are all the effects of this deceptively simple novel.)

Gestures and Mannerisms—The Actions of the Body

A brisk, confident stride or a shuffle; nails drummed against a table, hair twirled around a finger; narrowed eyes; a frown line etched between the brows; bitten lips. All these can dramatize either a characteristic stance toward the world or a transient emotional state.

People sometimes try to hide a physical characteristic with gestures, or lack of them: They won't smile because they're ashamed of their teeth, or they hunch over because they think they're too tall.

Similarly, people call attention to traits they want others to notice: fluffing their hair or waving graceful hands.

Certain illnesses and learning disabilities can manifest themselves in gestures: an autistic child who rubs a ball between his palms, or a sufferer of Parkinson's disease with shaking hands.

In a restaurant, watch people at the next table talk, when they're too far away for you to make out the words. See how they rearrange silverware, hide their mouths behind napkins, hold their coffee cups. How might any of these gestures underscore how they're communicating—a story exaggerated, an apology offered, a favor asked?

Through Clothing and Appearance—The Action of Choosing a Wardrobe

A brunette who bleaches her hair blonde; a teenager who shaves it off; a man with six gold chains disappearing into the hair on his chest; an elderly woman in support hose.

Think how Jenny Fields (Garp's mother in *The World According to Garp*) always wore her nurse's uniform. Miss Havisham (in Dickens's *Great Expectations*) always wore her wedding dress.

A woman wearing a plain gold band is different from the one wearing a three-karat diamond wedding set. Maybe she's poorer. Or maybe she's not very acquisitive, or doesn't want to advertise her wealth. (I know an enormously wealthy woman who wears a plain gold band.)

A woman living on the streets dresses differently than a woman in a corporate boardroom.

As they might with gestures, people use makeup and clothing to draw attention to or to hide different physical characteristics: wearing black to look thinner or more striking; platform shoes to look taller; a hat to cover a bald spot.

People use their wardrobe to seduce, intimidate, impress or blend in. They wear clothes to reflect their cultural heritage.

Through Their Surroundings—The Action of Decorating

To the extent that people decorate their living and work environments, those choices reflect their characters as well.

A home with six TV sets is different from the home with six encyclopedias (not to say one house can't have both).

These days a car is a kind of living environment for many people. Does your character have zebra seat covers? What stations would you hear when you pressed the buttons on his car radio?

An executive who has four pictures of his wife in his office is different from the executive who has four pictures of his sailboat.

Let me use the subject of decor as another opportunity to observe how an author creates a richer character by showing and not telling. The executive with pictures of his wife or his sailboat in his office is a richer character than the one about whom we are told, "John really loved his wife," or "John really loved his sailboat."

The detail of the pictures is open to interpretation. The executive with the pictures of his wife may be overcompensating because he works such long hours that the only time he sees his wife is when he looks at those pictures. The executive with the pictures of the boat may not even be interested in sailing; he might just be trying to impress his boss who's a sailing freak.

Here are two different descriptions of the same room:

FIRST VERSION:

It was obvious he was single. Not that the space was slovenly; it was actually reasonably neat, but it was utilitarian, and emotionally Spartan, in a way few women would care for.

Never mind the controversial practice of ending a sentence with a preposition. Although this description contains a worthwhile insight about the differing tastes of women and men, the description is also very "told" to us, rather than shown. Certain conclusions have been reached about the room, but we can't see the room at all.

SECOND VERSION:

The room was small and the only lamp was on a scratched-up desk of unfinished pine. Two of the walls were lined with bookshelves fashioned from bricks and planks. The hardwood floors had been recently cleaned, but the two throw rugs were worn so thin that the fabric was shiny.

We might surmise: Whoever uses this room mostly sits at the desk; he's clean and he cares about books but either doesn't have money for furniture or doesn't care to spend money on it.

But we might surmise any number of other things, too. What's important is that we can experience the room; we are in it. When an author creates an experience for the reader to share, then the author and the reader are partners. The author is doing her work but leaving plenty for the reader to do as well.

This illustration about showing and telling can apply to all of the categories just discussed. It is preferable to give us actual dialogue along the lines of, "Just shut your mouth," instead of telling us, "He was often nasty." It is preferable for us to see a character's eye twitch than to read, "She was nervous."

Through Personal Philosophy—The Action of Belief

Christian or Buddhist? Marxist or Capitalist? Your characters should not be mouthpieces for a philosophy, but how we answer the big question says a lot about how we view ourselves and others. (It should also say something about how we treat each other, and it does, but not always the way it should.)

Many of us grow up to believe what our parents did, or to embrace the dominant beliefs systems of our culture. But maybe your character has found her own way, or finds a new one in the course of your novel. What would make a Presbyterian become a Catholic, or an anarchist start voting Republican?

Physical Appearance

In *How to Write a Damn Good Novel,* James N. Frey asked,

Where would Jim Thorpe have been . . . had he been born with a club foot? Or Marilyn Monroe, had she turned out flat-chested? Or Hank Aaron, had he had a withered arm? Or Barbra Streisand, a small voice?

> . . . A petite, delicate, golden-haired girl with big blue eyes grows up with a completely different set of expectations about what she's going to get out of life than her needle-nosed, bug-eyed sister.

You may not relish this reference to our culture's emphasis on female beauty, but you can hardly deny its truth, nor the reality that our faces and bodies affect how we feel about ourselves, as well as our choice of profession, hobbies, love interests and friends.

If our bodies help shape our souls, then our souls, eventually, start to shape our bodies. The old saying has it that when you're young you have the face your parents gave you; when you're old you have the face you earn. Oil of Olay notwithstanding, one can see the lines of one's character etched into one's face over the years: the pinched mouth or the laugh lines.

Actually, physical appearance is a kind of gray area between action and luck. We can't choose how tall we are, or the natural color of our hair. But we can affect our own appearance to a great extent. Sometimes a person becomes overweight because he's lonely and fills his hours through eating; or overly thin in an obsessive search for perfection. When a guy has a tan it might mean he's a construction worker or that he has the leisure time to travel to the South of France. A prizefighter's face starts to show signs of his profession after a few years. Some men grow beards; some men get manicures.

Describing a character physically for the reader is also important in letting us picture the action of the novel. That doesn't mean we need to know the circumference of every joint. Your job will be to select the most interesting and relevant details of a character's appearance, and let us imagine the rest.

When describing a character physically, it's particularly effective to weave that description into the action; doing so immediately makes the description more memorable.

Let's say we're first introduced to your 6'9" character as he tries to squeeze into a coach seat on a flight to Cincinnati.

Or a very attractive person enters a room and all members of the opposite sex turn to look.

Or you might describe a suspect's face from the point of view of a detective as he scrutinizes her for signs of guilt.

Still More Ways to Reveal Character

The following ways that characters reveal themselves are not really actions, but they are important devices for characterization.

Heritage

We don't choose our parents' background but that, too, affects us.

Think of the experience of entire generations born in America to immigrant parents who came looking for a better way of life. Think of the children of Brahmins, the children of pariahs.

When you describe a character as the daughter of sharecroppers you tell us something different than if you told us that she was the daughter of a Vegas showgirl, or the daughter of a United States Senator. Maybe any one of them could become the first woman president of the United States, but they will travel down very different roads to the White House.

Pip, the hero of Dickens's *Great Expectations*, is motivated largely by his desire to escape his working class antecedents.

The eponymous hero of George Eliot's *Daniel Deronda* is kept as a child from knowing who his mother is, since she is an actress, and a Jew.

Social Milieu (The Values of the Time and Place)

Like it or not, we're also shaped by the values of the time and place in which we live.

Scarlett O'Hara sees nothing wrong with owning slaves because her parents and every other white person who can afford it does.

In *The Scarlet Letter*, Hester Prynne is ostracized for bearing a child out of wedlock. If she'd lived in San Francisco in the 1990s, she would have been respected for choosing an alternate lifestyle.

She also would have been eligible for a number of support services. And, being the seamstress she was, she might have started her own line of sportswear, called *Hester!*

The protagonist of Jay McInerney's novel, *Bright Lights, Big City*, is set adrift in the world of New York nightlife, where drug abuse and casual sex are the norms.

Usually our parents (or whomever is charged with raising us), embody the values of the larger society. Sometimes they rebel and encourage us to follow. Obviously characters don't always conform to society's expectations; some of the most interesting ones won't. But that will say a lot about them, too.

The influence of social milieu on characters (and through them, on plot) is one reason why so many novels are successfully set during times of social upheaval (the American Civil War, the Russian or French Revolutions, Germany before or during the Holocaust). All bets are off. The old ways don't work anymore, and characters discover just how adaptable they are—or aren't.

Personal History

By personal history, I'm referring to everything that happened to your character or that your character did before the novel begins. All these experiences—illnesses, the loss of loved ones, a gold medal in Olympic figure skating—have further shaped him. Therefore it's valuable for you as the author to be intimately familiar with a character's background.

But the past is by definition less interesting than the present, unless it's part of the story, too. That's why, in *Get That Novel Started!*, I warned against using long flashbacks to motivate characters, or "to tell what they're like," as students often protest they must do. Such flashbacks, when they serve *only* to characterize, without furthering the story, tend to bog down the novel. Flashbacks are static.

However, a brief and pithy *reference to the character's past* can accomplish at least two things effectively: It can help us put that character into a larger social context, and show us more aspects of the character's personality before the present story will.

Let's say your character is a middle-aged woman named Esther. She's walking into a fancy reception at the Plaza Hotel with her husband.

Esther checked her coat, her best one with the fox-fur collar. *Nicer than my mother ever saw.* Esther's mother had grown up on the lower East Side, the daughter of Polish immigrants who never learned to speak English.

It's one sentence, but it tells us a lot about Esther, about how she might feel at a fancy-schmancy party at the Plaza.

A reference to the past can be specific and visual, too. Suppose you continued on:

> One day her mother sent her out with rags to sell. Esther's only good skirt, a pleated red plaid, was in the pile.

End of reference to the past. It's connected through a strong association to the present (what clothes Esther can afford) and it distills a life into one moment.

As the present-time scene continues and Esther socializes with other people at the reception, what we know of her background gives us a lens to look through. The author might include such a reference to the past for just that reason: so that we can see a character's actions in a certain light. Perhaps if we see Esther being just a little bit boastful about her new car, or her son in prep school, we'll forgive her, now that we know she once had to sell her only good skirt.

What would be far less effective would be to make an entire scene of the skirt-selling. It's in the past and it's only purpose would be to characterize Esther. Novels must be much denser than that, each scene accomplishing many things.

Writers are often tempted to give readers the life story of their characters in opening chapters, and it rarely works (one must never say never). But there's something else you can accomplish with a *brief* journey back in time.

Let's say that you're writing a novel about a young resident in a big city hospital. In the opening chapter Young Res is working the emergency room. We watch as he treats the victims and perpetrators of crime, substance abuse and domestic violence. Meanwhile, he hasn't slept in thirty-six hours. So it's understandable that Young Res is feeling bitter about his job, cynical toward humanity and impatient with his staff.

You want us to like Young Res, but the fact is that we're going to see him be a real grouch for the duration of the chapter. A reference to the past or two would be one way to show us some other sides of him quickly.

> Young Res looked down at the semi-conscious old bum on the stretcher. *Another guy from the street. Wonder if he'll last the night.*

Young Res had come a long way since the first time he knew he wanted to be a doctor. That was when he was eight, and his sister had been rushed to the hospital, crying with a pain in her stomach. Young Res had watched her drive off with their father and prayed, *Please God, let her be all right.*

Young Res pushed hair back off his sweaty forehead and said to the nurse, "Check all his vitals and line up a room for him upstairs. Stat!"

The reference to Young Res's earlier desire to help the sick balances his current fatigue and cynicism. Once again, it's a specific incident, shown, not told. *And it's short.*

There are several ways in which writers—sometimes even very experienced ones—lapse into telling about characters, when they could be showing. As we'll see, these include devices that can be effective when used sparingly and correctly, as well as devices that a writer should generally avoid.

Interior Monologue—Its Uses and Abuses

Beginning writers in particular have a fondness for characterization through reflection or introspection. I believe the term is "interior monologue," a term that has always grated on my nerves, but then, I have a low threshold for anxiety.

Here's some interior monologue:

> Chuck lay on the couch pressing the buttons on the remote control. He wondered what to do with his life. Ever since graduating from college two years previously, he had spent his days lying right here, with the remote, watching *Oprah, Geraldo, Donahue, Yolanda.*
>
> *I could be on one of those shows,* he thought. *I could tell everyone MY story and then the world would listen. How I did all the things my parents told me to do. Went to school, studied hard, even majored in business! I graduated number four out of a class of a hundred and twenty-seven, but look at me now! My wife Dottie is typing some jerk executive's correspondence, and I can't find a job. . . . And I've tried! I swear I've tried! How many interviews have I been on? Three? Three hundred? But as soon as they see my big nose they turn away. I know I'm being discriminated against because of my nose. . . .*

Interior monologue is a legitimate way of sneaking in a little first person point of view, for the sake of color, in a third person novel.

It has its place—especially when the character's voice is energetic, specific, interesting—as a way of getting to know the character.

But don't rely on it, either for characterization or to give us information, in preference to dramatic scenes. By dramatic scenes I don't necessarily mean scenes in which tears are shed and furniture thrown (though there's nothing like having a couch sail through a window to liven up a dull novel), but rather, scenes in which characters are striving toward their goals and interacting in vivid ways.

Regarding poor Chuck, bitter and unemployed, imagine a scene in which he is packing his wife's lunch when she comes downstairs. "Honey," she ventures, "you're not going to sit home all day watching the talk shows again, are you?"

"What if I am?" Chuck asks sullenly, and then absently rubs the tip of his nose.

The scene can go on from there, perhaps escalating into an argument as Chuck's wife tries to convince him that he's really got to get over this nose hang-up.

The interior monologue gives us static information about Chuck's current trouble. The scene with Chuck's wife can give us the same information while also showing us who Chuck's wife is and how they interact with each other. And a character acting is almost always better than a character thinking.

Showing and Telling in Narration and Scene

We've already had occasion to refer to scenes as an element of the novel. We'll have many more occasions, so let's define scene, and its counterpart, narration, for our purposes now and for the rest of this book.

Think of a scene in a novel as being similar to a scene in a play. It is action that unfolds before our eyes in a way that approximates real time. We see what the characters are doing, hear what they hear, smell what they smell.

Not everything, of course. After all, at any one moment, you are not aware of *everything* going on around you. You may be conscious of the stiffness in your neck but not of the fly in the next room. You may notice a darker square on the wall where a picture has recently been removed but not register the Sears-issue carpet.

As a novelist, your job is to simulate reality, through the number and kind of details you select, so that we feel that we're there and know what's going on. Of course, since you as author are selecting what to show us (the leaky roof, the peeling paint) you are also able to influence, if not determine, our experience of it.

The important parts of your story should be dramatized in scenes: the confrontations, battles, first kisses, weddings and births, not necessarily in that order.

However, narration (sometimes called "summary") is an indispensable part of a novel as well. Without it—if you had to describe everything that happens to each character in a scene—your novel would be a thousand pages long, just getting your heroine out of bed and dressed in the morning. Narration is what gets you from scene to scene; in other words, from important event to important event.

Narration compresses time. An author can use narration to hit the high points of the story while eliminating information that is uninteresting or irrelevant.

Let's say you're writing a novel about a lifelong friendship between two women who meet in high school. Then you come to a part in which the two women live in different towns for a year. You want to convey the flavor of that year—their missing each other, the experiences they have on their own—but you also want to speed through it because the book is about their relationship, not about their time apart.

What you do is narrate, giving us just what we need to know.

> The year passed slowly for Ellen. She particularly hated the harsh Minnesota winter weather, unused to serious winters as she was. She didn't drive and was often stuck at home. So she would pass the afternoon writing to her dear friend Paula in Dallas.

As the passage above shows, narration can also be used to describe events that occur repeatedly: in this case, many afternoons spent writing letters.

A scene is a more natural way to show us characters, because we are seeing them closer up, in real time. A man comes home, throws his briefcase on the floor, yells at his wife, "Where's my damn dinner?"

Or the warrior queen gathers her advisors around her. "We must show our enemies no mercy," she announces.

By contrast, narration pushes you in the direction of telling rather than showing, because narration itself is more told and less shown than are scenes. In the passage above we are told that Ellen hated the winter weather rather than having an opportunity to see her struggle to put on layers of outerwear or curse the snow as it falls from the sky.

Now, it's hardly fatal to a novel to write, "Ellen hated the winter weather," but it is good to be aware how, even in narration, it is possible to do more showing than telling.

Max was a terrible shopper, and finally his wife wouldn't go to the department store with him any more.

This is telling. But try it this way:

Whenever Max went to Nieman-Marcus, he'd insult the salesmen with some remark like, "I can't believe you're selling these suits for six hundred dollars. I wouldn't let my dog wear them, even if he *was* a thirty-two regular."

You can see why his wife might decline to join him after that.

The second example is still narration: It summarizes an event. But it shows rather than tells us that Max was a terrible shopper. A scene would dramatize this still more effectively, but you also have to weigh whether or not Max's obnoxious behavior at Nieman-Marcus warrants an entire scene in the context of the novel as a whole.

Words Not to Live By

By now you may have noticed that there's a type of word you want to avoid both in scene and narration. These are "telling" words or, you might say, "conclusion," or "value judgment" words. Words like: good, bad, pretty, awful, great, terrible, nice, wonderful, mean, fantastic and splendid.

Stereotypes: A Quick but Painful Way to Kill the Reader's Interest

James N. Frey points out that many characters are of recognizable *types*. "But there is an enormous difference between fresh characters of a recognizable type and stereotyped characters."

Almost anyone can be categorized as a type: A rebellious teenager, a precocious child, a philandering husband. We may be different types in different areas of our life: an overprotective mother, an eccentric writer, a whiny wife, a hard-headed businesswoman.

Once again, you may use a type as a starting point. You *need* a crusty but good-hearted head nurse for your hospital. Fine. Start with that, and then go ahead and fill in the details. Soon, crusty but good-hearted nurse will be Felicia, forty-eight, a widow who's never found anyone to equal Joe, the husband who died in a zamboni accident, and who spends all those extra hours at the hospital because that's where she feels the most needed, and who has Joe's name tattooed on her shoulder. . . . In short, she'll be a person, not just a type.

Any character who does not exhibit specific and individual traits, or whose individual traits are too familiar, is in danger of becoming a stereotype: the cookie-baking Grandma, the angelic child with blond ringlets, the gunslinger in the black hat. Whether you want to convey innocence, evil or strength, you not only must find the details, you have to find details that haven't been overused.

Most of us know to avoid certain ethnic stereotypes. We certainly should, anyway. Please, no Jewish mothers, Italian gangsters or Irish beat cops with cheerful brogues.

But you should also watch out for the new stereotypes: the evil corporate executive who's polluting the environment, the sexist husband who won't let his wife work.

Such people exist, obviously, but when they appear in your novel you must also make them individuals. Don't rely on the current public outrage against male chauvinist pigs to make the character interesting. Why does *this particular husband* not want his wife to work? What does *this particular* corporate executive tell himself to rationalize the dumping of toxic waste into the Mississippi?

When you use stereotypes you are not only telling rather than showing, you are making a value judgment about an entire character, rather than letting us see that character and decide how we feel for ourselves.

No one in your own life, whom you know more than passingly, is a stereotype, although there may be some types. So, to avoid stereotypes in your fiction, and to find ways of showing rather than telling, there's a fairly simple rule to follow. *Get to know your characters as thoroughly as possible.*

Here's how:

Getting to Know Them

First of all, let's acknowledge that fictional characters are just that: invented personalities inhabiting invented bodies. You make them up.

But we writers are less clinical than that. Even before you start writing your novel, you probably have mystical feelings about your characters, as if they dwelt in a hazy limbo, and you just had to bring them out into the light.

Let's go with that. Imagine your characters already *are* people— you don't have to make them up, you have to get to know them. Because once you know them then you'll *know* what kind of clothes they wear, what their favorite colors are, how fast they can run, whether they can drive a stick shift. You'll be able to convey them through those details to the reader.

You may have strong feelings about someone right away, but forming a deep relationship takes time. Getting to know your characters is just like getting to know people in real life. You need to hang out with them, observe, ask a few questions. Taking time to get to know them is the difference between a first date and a fiftieth wedding anniversary. So be patient and do your homework.

Here are some exercises to do. They are roughly in recommended order, but don't worry about the order; just do them.

Do them most of all for your main character but do them (or at least some of them) for all the characters who play significant roles.

The Character Bio

Your main character is a young woman of nineteen who arrives from Dublin to work for a year as a nanny in America.

The first thing you do is write her biography.

> Sibhoan was born in Dublin on March 4, 1977. She was the third daughter of her parents, Alice and Gerald McKay. Sibhoan went to Catholic School where her favorite teacher was Sister Theresa, who exuded a gentle spirituality and taught Sibhoan that. . . .

Go on for ten to fifteen pages. Yes, go on. Maybe you don't know a lot about growing up in Dublin. You don't have to travel to Ireland; find someone who did grow up in Dublin who can tell you about it, or read books by people who describe growing up in Ireland.

They say we're all separated by no more than six people who know each other. What that means to you as a writer is that you can find out most of what you need to know by asking people you know, and if they don't know, asking them if they know someone who does.

When you do a bio, don't get too bogged down in the story of the character's parents, let alone how Grandpa Sam homesteaded the family ranch. Sure, everything you learn about a character is useful, but more recent events will tend to be more relevant to the novel you are writing.

And *do not* feel that you have to reprint everything you discover about your character in your novel. The bio is primarily to help you and your character get acquainted. It will likely provide you with a couple of ideas for those mini-flashbacks or references to the past we talked about. But maybe the reader will never know anything about the character's past. That might be OK, too.

And even though you may not include much (or even anything) from the bio in the novel itself, the character biography is still the first and fundamental character-developing exercise.

The Interview

Another useful tool is the interview. This is where you sit down at your typewriter and pretend that you are a journalist interviewing your character. But don't just be any journalist—be an obnoxious, prying one who won't let your character get away with avoiding anything.

> Donna: "So, Emma, just how long do you think you're going to get away with these trips to Rouen before your husband suspects?"
>
> Madame Bovary: "Donna, Charles is such a dolt, he's *never* going to catch on."

The Monologue

Whether or not your novel is written in first person, you can write monologues for your characters in which they vent their feelings and bestow their observations about the action of the novel, the other characters in it (most important), their own histories and the human condition in general.

> My husband's dullness oppresses me. When I married him I believed that I would inspire him to accomplish something fine. I could see that he loved me. But now I understand that love is different for everyone and that Charles's has limits. He can't see beyond our little house and our little village. He doesn't want more. I do.

Do it for a good five pages or more.

They've Got a Secret

Novelist and teacher Thomas Trebitsch Parker shared with me an exercise that he gives to his own students. "When developing a character, ask yourself what that character's most closely guarded secret is. That will quickly take you to deeper parts of that character than the usual vital stats about siblings and income."

We all have a few things that we don't want other people to know about us. Those might include sexual practices or a crime, but they could also be eating binges, a hand-washing compulsion, or just our true feelings.

Determining that secret may lead you to plot possibilities, as we'll see, or you may choose to keep your character's confidence. Your character may resent you for knowing so much about him, but that's his problem.

Let the Character Write Her Own Obituary

I was part of a group listening to writer and teacher Gregg Levoy talk about the business of writing when another member of the audience expressed both her desire to, and fear of, embarking on a career as a freelance writer.

Levoy suggested she do an exercise that some existential psychologists use: write her own obituary.

The woman seemed a bit shaken up at the notion, but in fact, writing one's own obituary is an effective way quickly to determine what you'd most like to do with your life. Doing it may be harder, but fortunately, that's beyond the scope of this book.

Meanwhile, put yourself in the head of your character and let her do the same exercise for herself. Maybe your character still thinks it's possible to become a prima ballerina even though she's forty and has never taken a dance lesson. Or maybe he imagines himself dying alone and unloved when in fact many friends would be bereft.

As with determining the character's most closely guarded secret (or secrets), this exercise can help you penetrate more quickly to what the character wants and how he perceives himself. He, too, may find it a bit nerve-wracking, but it will force him to confront himself—and you, him.

Lists

It's a good idea to do character exercises before you start writing the novel. But you may also find that you need to go back and do more of them later, after the novel is well underway. Making lists about characters, besides being a helpful exercise, is also a good *variation* of other exercises—as a novelist, you're always looking for ways to keep yourself interested in your own work throughout the long process of writing a novel.

Just as in any relationship, you're always discovering new things about your characters. Making lists about them is a good way to deepen your acquaintance. The information you come up with will overlap with other exercises but that's OK.

• *List the last five entries in the character's check register.* This is a bourgeois exercise: it assumes that a character is middle-class and

has a checkbook. But do it if it applies.
- *List ten items in the character's shopping cart.*
- *List five or more items in this character's purse, briefcase or school locker.*
- *List the last three books the character read.* Maybe it was a mystery series. Maybe it was the complete works of Henry James. Some people read more than others. It may be that the last book the character read was *Dick and Jane Go to School.*
- *Make up your own variations of these lists.* The last five restaurants the character went to; her five favorite cities; the five foods he or she would take to a desert island.

Get Your Writing Group Involved

Several writing groups have emerged from classes I've taught, which I mention because it makes me very proud.

One particular group told me how they instituted a system whereby each week, at least one of them would fax the others in the voice of his or her protagonist. Even more interestingly, the members of the group sometimes imagined that their protagonists met each other.

The illusion that your characters actually exist may not be enough to make them real to your reader, but it's not a bad place to start. The more real they are to you, the more you want to give them life so that others can know them, too.

When they start hiding your socks, maybe then you should worry.

An Added Bonus to Expending All This Effort

Everything in a novel is connected to everything else. Even though you won't use all the material that you come up with in these exercises, they will aid you in many aspects of the novel. Writing biographies, making lists, asking questions etc., will give you more plot ideas, insights into other characters and help you discover motifs you want to develop further. Doing character exercises is a lot of work, but so is writing a novel.

Sources of Inspiration

The most common source of inspiration for creating characters is your own life. No problem there. You already know a lot about yourself and the people around you, and you're probably already interested in yourself and them. Go ahead and put all your pals in your books. You should still do exercises to organize for yourself what you know about these truth-inspired fictional characters. And then, when you put them in fictional, or even fiction*alized* situations, they will take on lives of their own.

You can also look at historical figures, famous people or other fictional characters. A lot of writers have tried to reproduce Holden Caulfield, the hero of J.D. Salinger's *Catcher in the Rye*. When such homage is paid cynically, in the attempt to cash in on another author's success, it usually fails, as when Alexandra Ripley tried to duplicate Scarlett O'Hara for the limp sequel to Margaret Mitchell's book. But to use someone else's creation as a starting point is fair enough.

If you have a background or interest in psychology, you can start out with what you know about personality types described by the enneagram, or disorders documented in the *DSM-IV*. Even the signs of the zodiac, or the animals of the Chinese zodiac, can provide personality profiles that are jumping-off places. "Whatever works" is generally my motto, in life as well as writing.

Bear in mind that characters who are meant to represent philosophies (the existentialist, the libertarian) will not be "whole and alive, their breath congealing on the page"; they will be mouthpieces. That doesn't mean that you can't show us what kind of people espouse certain convictions, as long as they are people first.

THE FINER POINTS

We've discussed many of the ways that characters reveal who they are to the reader. But what assures us as writers that readers will be interested in what they discover?

There are three qualities with which you must endow your characters in order to ensure you compel our interest. The first two are complexity and stature. The third has two parts: a strong goal and the ability to act upon it.

As we'll see, the requirements of complexity, stature and the ability to act upon a goal are relative to the character's importance in the novel. But let's start by talking about main characters, for whom these qualities are the most crucial.

Complexity's the Thing: A Look at *Anna Karenina*

Complexity is what makes a character interesting and lifelike.

Think of the people whom you know well. You may love them or hate them, but I doubt there's anyone with whom you are truly intimate (as readers should be with a main character) whom you see as all good or all bad.

In fiction, even the greatest heroes have flaws: Superman is afraid of commitment. Sherlock Holmes has that little cocaine habit. Oedipus has *hubris*.

It is of equal importance that your villains be more than just mighty forces of evil if you want them to be truly compelling. (Granted, villains are rarely the *main* main characters, but they often play important roles.)

I once read a biography of Adolf Hitler. The book included some fond accounts from his servants during the last days of World War II, describing him as gently expressing concern for their personal welfare. Now, Adolf Hitler as a man capable of gentleness is far more terrifying than Adolf Hitler as pure screaming maniac. As screaming maniac, he's just a force of nature, like Hurricane Andrew. Hurricane Andrew may do a lot of damage, but it's not a character; it makes no choices about where it goes or whom it destroys.

When we see a villain as a human being, responsible for his actions, capable of making different choices, we respond with deeper emotions than we would to the description of the destructive force of a hurricane. We potentially see ourselves.

To illustrate complex characterization, let's look at Leo Tolstoy's masterpiece *Anna Karenina*. If I had to choose one book that all novelists should read, *Anna Karenina* would be the one, for several reasons, but most of all because of that very complexity of characterization.

Since this is a novel we'll refer to several more times, let me summarize it briefly.

Anna Karenina is a beautiful Russian aristocrat who is resignedly married to the upright, but uptight, government minister, Alexey Karenin. Early in the novel she meets the dashing Count Vronsky, who falls in love with her as only a Russian officer can fall in love with a woman, and who finally seduces her. When Anna's husband discovers her affair he tells her to stop, or at least not to shame him by publicly displaying her infidelity. But it's a bit late for that, because Anna is pregnant.

After Anna and Vronksy's baby, a daughter, is born, and Anna herself nearly dies from a post-partum illness, she leaves her husband so that she can live with Vronsky. However, she can't quite bring herself to get a divorce, which would legally separate her from the son she had with Karenin.

But now that Vronsky and Anna have what they want—each other—they find it rather empty, although neither dares articulate that, even to themselves. They travel; Vronsky paints without passion; they return to Russia where Anna discovers that the old double standard shuts her out from society while still granting Vronsky access. As pressures mount, including Vronksy's mother's scheme to get him to marry another woman, Anna convinces herself (not completely without cause) that Vronsky is tired of her. Pursuing him to a railway station, in a moment of impulsive despair, she throws herself under the wheels of a train.

The three principals of this part of the story, then, are Anna, Vronksy and Anna's husband, Alexey Karenin. Anna is an affectionate, charming woman trapped in a loveless marriage to a man whose idea of a good time is paring his fingernails. Anna resists Vronsky's advances but the intensity of those advances, combined with her vulnerability, cause her to succumb.

Vronsky truly loves her. He resigns his commission in the army so that they can be together. When Anna leaves her husband, Vronsky wishes to legalize their relationship so that his daughter and their future children will bear his name. Meanwhile, Karenin is not only incapable of giving Anna the emotional support that would have ensured her loyalty from the beginning, once he learns of her betrayal he treats her vindictively, barring her from seeing her son.

At first glance, then, Anna is the heroine, Vronsky the hero, and Anna's husband Alexey Karenin the villain. But Tolstoy's characters actually defy such categorization.

Vronsky is short-sighted and selfish. According to the code by which he lives, Tolstoy tells us, the feelings of husbands don't exist. But in the end, Anna's don't, either. Vronsky seduces her without the ability to comprehend what she risks by loving him. Throughout the novel he chafes at the restrictions she places upon him.

Alexey Karenin is indeed sarcastic and rigid. He's also a weak man in many respects, who's protected himself from having to experience any true feeling by adhering to abstract notions of duty. Rules must be obeyed, appearances maintained.

But from Karenin's own point of view, he hasn't been a bad husband. He works hard and keeps Anna in ballgowns. They have a child and a respectable position in society. All of a sudden Anna's flaunting her affair with an army officer! Where did he go wrong?

After Anna's daughter is born, Karenin actually saves the baby's life when he discovers that the wet nurse has no milk. And at the end of the novel, when Anna is dead and the stunned Vronsky has rejoined the army, it is Karenin who once again takes Anna's daughter in.

As for Anna, we sympathize with her from the beginning, when she first arrives in Moscow from St. Petersburg to repair a quarrel between her brother and sister-in-law. She is full of affectionate talk about the little boy she left behind. And when Vronsky first declares himself, she insists that it must never be.

Yet she has many moments of pettiness and manipulativeness, as when she flirts with another woman's husband just to see if she can. She punishes herself with her indecision about her future while knowing the result of her indecision will also punish others. And she's unable to form the kind of bond with her daughter that she has with her son by Karenin.

In *The Art of the Novel*, Milan Kundera writes,

> Religions and ideologies . . . can cope with the novel only by translating its language of relativity and ambiguity into their own . . . dogmatic discourse. They require that someone be right: Either Anna Karenina is the victim of a narrow-minded tyrant, or Karenin is the victim of an immoral woman. . . .

What requires courage (according to Kundera) is to

> . . . take the world as ambiguity, to be obliged to face not just a single absolute truth but a welter of contradictory truths (truths embodied in *imaginary selves* called *characters*), to have as one's only certainty *the wisdom of uncertainty*. . . ."

Let preachers and idealogues have simple answers. We're *novelists*.

Remember that complex characters are multidimensional. They are capable of a variety of responses to a variety of situations; they can make a lot of things happen. And by the way, the more you show, and don't tell, the more complex they'll be.

Stature

Stature is what makes a character admirable.

We can summarize stature by quoting the well-known expression, "He's the fastest gun in the west."

Traditionally, fictional characters had stature because they were larger-than-life, that is, the bravest, brightest, most resourceful or cutest person in the whole wide world. Helen of Troy has stature because she's the most beautiful woman. Hercules because he's the strongest man. Robin Hood because he's the best archer.

Modernly, some genres still demand a character who is larger-than-life. The heroine of a romance novel is rarely a plain woman with a good personality: She's more likely to be exceptionally beautiful. A sweeping historical epic about the Germanic tribes invading Rome calls for a mighty warrior to lead them, someone bigger, better, smarter and stronger than ordinary mortals.

Popular fiction in general also remains fascinated with people of high status: movie stars, oil barons and, yes, royalty. After all, one of the reasons people read is for pure entertainment, and what better way to escape your own banal existence than to imagine yourself an English princess royal, surrounded by devoted servants and every possible luxury, only heartbroken that your brother the king is trying to force you to marry the old French king when you're in love with a dashing commoner. . . .

Being a king or a queen, being the strongest or the most beautiful in the world, gives a character stature. Now, in modern realistic fiction, a main character doesn't have to be Hercules or Helen. But he or she *does* still need stature.

You endow a character with stature whenever you give that character superior qualities, not just external ones like strength or beauty, but intelligence, humor, compassion or even the ability to play a mean game of chess.

Cyrano de Bergerac is an ugly guy with a big nose. But he has stature because he's a fine poet, a skilled swordsman and really brave in battle.

The hardboiled detective popularized by Dashiell Hammett (and enjoying quite a renaissance now in mystery novels) is usually broke, at least a borderline alcoholic, and the keeper of dubious company. His resourcefulness, his moral code and the soft side he keeps hidden give him stature.

Stature can also emerge as the accumulation of a number of choices on the part of a character, or even, sometimes, as the result of one dramatic act.

Cyrano de Bergerac has been writing letters to his beloved Roxane under the name of the handsome Christian. Christian realizes that Roxane has fallen in love not with him, but with the writer of the letters, and demands that Cyrano tell her the truth and make her choose between the two men. Before Cyrano can rally his nerve, Christian is mortally wounded in battle (he may have exposed himself to death rather than lose Roxane). Cyrano whispers to the dying Christian that Roxane has chosen him. His desire to help Christian die in peace adds to his stature.

Jean Valjean, the hero of Victor Hugo's *Les Miserables*, has been pursued for fifteen years by police inspector Javert, who wishes to send him back to prison for a piddling crime. Javert's pursuit has forced Valjean to live in fear for a good part of his life. But when Valjean is actually charged by a band of rebels with the job of executing Javert, Valjean instead sets him free. Nice stature boost, to a man who already has a lot.

I'd like to think we all have stature, if someone takes the time to find it in us. And as a novelist, you must find it for each of your important characters.

Stature is the most elusive concept of the three we'll discuss. It's easy to see how traditional heroes have it. But it isn't difficult to find examples of modern-day protagonists who at first glance seem to have no real stature. Take Maggie Moran, the main character of Anne Tyler's *Breathing Lessons*. Maggie is neither beautiful, brilliant, nor rich; she's no longer young. Take Holden Caulfield, the protagonist of J.D. Salinger's *Catcher in the Rye*: He's a fairly ordinary guy who can't even stay in school.

But Maggie Moran has stature because of her extraordinary compassion and love for others. Holden Caulfield has it because of his extreme sensitivity, his disgust for everything that is phony. Often modern protagonists derive their stature from their intelligence, level of insight or humor. But in order to succeed as a main character, that character must have at least some quality that sets him or her apart from ordinary people.

Off Their Duffs: A Driving Passion and the Ability to Act on It

A goal, and the ability to act on it, is what reveals a character to us and what drives the plot forward.

In real life many people are slow to make changes in their lives. They complain for years about their jobs, spouses, and old kitchens that need remodeling. "One of these days I'm going down to Home Depot to pick me up some new linoleum!" they declare, as another weekend slides by.

This may be realistic enough, but in a main character it won't make for very interesting reading, nor will it create many opportunities for you to get the plot moving.

We want to read about people who are able to take the helm of the ship of their lives, even if that ship is going down in a storm. What this means is that *a character should want something very badly and be able to take action to get it.*

Giving a character a goal is another way to show that character to us, rather than simply tell us about him. What a character wants reveals a lot about who that character is. To write, "She was materialistic," or "She was altruistic," is telling. But if we see that my driving passion, no pun intended, is to acquire a Mercedes, or to find a cure for cancer, that's showing.

And, as we'll discuss in chapter three, a character's goal is one of the primary vehicles you have of creating a plot.

In addition to these two important results, a goal that we can understand can make us root for a character even if that character isn't a nice person.

James N. Frey describes this process in *How to Write a Damn Good Novel II*: "Identification occurs when the reader . . . supports [the character's] goals and aspirations and has a strong desire that the character achieve them."

Jay Gatsby has gained his wealth through dubious means; there's a rumor that he's killed a man. But he loves Daisy so purely that anyone who's ever loved and lost (and who hasn't?) will root for him to get his heart's desire, even as we see it's impossible.

The main character of Fay Weldon's novel, *The Life and Loves of a She-Devil*, is Ruth, an overweight, unattractive woman whose husband has abandoned her for a selfish, pretty writer of trash fiction. So, although Ruth takes no end of bizarre, vindictive measures against them both, we still root for her, so desirous are we that she get her revenge.

Say you're writing about a domineering mother who's trying to control the life of her daughter, meanwhile lying to her husband to keep him from getting involved in their disagreements. Even though the mother may be scheming and deceptive, her daughter may be an incompetent weirdo who, without intervention, is destined to end up trimming the beard of some religious cult figure. We would support the mother's goal to help her daughter.

As a final benefit, a character who wants something passionately and is trying hard to get it will simply be more interesting to read about. People without goals are boring. And people who want things but never go after them get pretty darn annoying after a while. I mean, aren't you tired of hearing your sister threaten to dump her boyfriend? Don't you just wish she'd *do* it already?

Likable Characters: Nice Work if You Can Get It

You will often hear that it's important to make characters in general, and main characters in particular, likable. And in fact it is a great advantage. Of course it's more palatable to read about someone

appealing than about someone who's disagreeable, selfish and sarcastic without even being funny. So as an author you certainly make
life a little easier on yourself by creating a likable main character,
a topic I addressed briefly in *Get That Novel Started!*

However, it is actually of more importance that you create a
character who is sufficiently complex, with enough stature, and the
ability to act on her goal. Melanie Hamilton is much more likable
than Scarlett O'Hara, but who'd want her as the main character, in
preference to Scarlett? Who'd want to see Amelia Sedley, loyal
and ladylike, as the protagonist of *Vanity Fair* in preference to the
brilliantly amoral Becky Sharp? Even Anna Karenina is far from a
perfectly admirable heroine. Just being nice won't make a character
interesting.

Besides helping us identify with characters by giving them goals
we can root for, James N. Frey further points out that you can
make us *sympathize* with even unlikable characters by putting those
characters into some condition that will make us feel sorry for them.
That condition can be loneliness, poverty, sorrow, incarceration or
a really dull job—anything that the average human being shouldn't
have to suffer. We can still sympathize with a character who isn't
herself sympathetic.

A good example of this is from Dorothy Allison's *Bastard Out of
Carolina*. The main character is a child called Bone. Bone is no
saint: She's capable of being mean, and she even breaks into a
Woolworth's (although in the context of the novel we understand
her desire to do so). But from early in the novel she's placed in
jeopardy, because her stepfather abuses her. We sympathize with
her plight, even though, if we stopped to think about it, we'd probably discover that we don't like *her* very much.

One of the nice things about fictional characters is that, no matter
how fully developed they are in the book, we don't actually have
to live with them. In real life I might prefer to be married to a
reliable and slightly dull guy who works a steady job than to an
inventor who spends his weekends trying to perfect a perpetual
motion machine in the garage. But the guy in the garage is going
to be more interesting to read about.

Wuthering Heights stars two of literature's most unlikable—we
might even say fiendish—characters. *Play It as It Lays* stars one of
the most neurotic. The plays of August Strindberg are pretty
scarcely populated with anyone we'd want to know in real life.

Note, though, that an unlikable character, be that person a main character or a secondary character, is a less likely candidate for a first-person narrator.

Woody Allen and the Age of Anti-Heroes

It's hard for most of us to imagine the world that Ulysses and Helen of Troy lived in: the uncharted seas, the unknown edge of the earth. After all, we've not only mapped pretty much every square inch of the planet, we've seen photos of Venus.

Our territory has shrunk. Now we live in rabbit-hutch condominium towers, commute in rolling tin cans and hope a stray bullet won't find us on the freeway.

It's the age of anti-heroes.

Before we define anti-heroes, let's review the main character as hero. As we've seen, the traditional larger-than-life hero of classical fiction—Robin Hood, Sherlock Holmes—has made room for a hero of more modest dimensions: a man or woman of average status, perhaps quite ordinary in some respects, who nevertheless has stature in at least some areas, and therefore compels our interest. That's *enough* to be a hero or heroine.

An anti-hero, then, isn't just a character who isn't larger-than-life, who isn't a king or who isn't the fastest gun in the west. Many heroes are none of these things anymore. In fact, the anti-hero *does* possess the three elements of a hero or heroine: complexity, stature and the ability to act upon a goal. The problem is that the anti-hero doesn't have the correct abilities that would help her get what she wants, and the forces against her are too strong. Most of all, what distinguishes the anti-hero from the modern hero of more ordinary dimensions is that society itself is against her in some way.

Anti-heroes are not a recent phenomenon. One of the roles of the novelist is to observe and critique society, and the anti-hero helps him serve that purpose. Usually the anti-hero is a person of low status: poor, from a lower class family or even labeled a criminal or insane. In at least one case I can think of he's an insect (Gregor Samsa in *The Metamorphosis*). The anti-hero is downtrodden or victimized by society, though those social forces may also be embodied by particular individuals who exploit him.

The old-fashioned hero is brave, a leader, respected by all. The anti-hero is Everyperson. A hero can leap tall buildings in a single bound. The anti-hero takes the elevator.

An anti-hero must represent something that's gone wrong with society and yet still be someone with whom we can sympathize. So anti-heroes may be low in status, but they must still have some of that stature we've talked about.

Take Willy Loman, the protagonist of Arthur Miller's *Death of a Salesman.* He's an anti-hero, as even his name establishes for us ("low man"). Willy Loman lives in one of the most classless societies ever, and yet this very egalitarianism destroys him. Willy has bought into the American Dream. He believes that if he's likable and works hard that he'll succeed. But the system chews him up and as he gets older, prepares to spit him out. In the end, faced with financial ruin, Willy decides to kill himself so that his wife can collect on their only remaining asset: his life insurance. There is irony in the idea that in capitalist society, where everything's for sale, a man can sell even his life.

Willy Loman isn't exactly a role model for young businesspeople across the land. But although an anti-hero we can still admire him. His goal is to provide for his family—a noble goal—and he does it at the greatest possible cost, proving, if nothing else, that he has the ability to act.

Note, though, that *Death of a Salesman* isn't just an anti-capitalist diatribe. It's also a drama about failed ambition, about marriage and about fathers and sons.

The role of the anti-hero in modern fiction has gotten a new sheen in the past couple of decades or so from Woody Allen, with the persona he created through a number of films, including *Bananas*; *Play It Again, Sam*; *Love and Death*; *Annie Hall* and *Manhattan.*

This early Woody Allen persona (it's recently taken on different dimensions) isn't always poor, though he sometimes makes choices that keep him from getting rich. He's clumsy, unattractive, socially inept and phobic. The indignities he suffers are not great when compared to Willy Loman. But in the context of the films themselves, they're great enough. In the Woody Allen world, what worse fate than not having a date for New Year's Eve?

What makes the Woody Allen character a true anti-hero is that his existence is really a critique of the society that surrounds him, a society that values looks, money and hedonistic pleasures over the capacity to think and feel.

The people with whom the Woody Allen character must deal are (to generalize) shallow, ambitious, gullible—like the airhead journalist he dates once in *Annie Hall*, or like Yale, the friend who's cheating on his wife in *Manhattan.*

Like Willy, the Woody Allen character has goals and the ability to act upon them, although his *way* of acting on them is sometimes ill-conceived, as when he studiously arranges his apartment to impress a date. He's doing his best, but his best isn't good enough, just as Willy's isn't.

But most of all, the Woody Allen character is morally superior to the people who surround him. Self-satisfied, attractive people look down on him but Woody Allen knows that by spending a lifetime doing aerobics they're only pretending that they're not going to die someday, too.

So the fact that these self-satisfied people are successful while Woody Allen can't get a date is a great injustice, a humorous version of the injustice it is that Willy Loman can't retire in style.

Ironically, this nobility of spirit places the anti-hero—the downtrodden, victimized man or woman—*above* other people. Secretly, perhaps, many of us see ourselves as anti-heroes. I, for one, have little trouble identifying with Woody Allen.

Who's on First?—Distinguishing Between
Main and Secondary Characters

Creating a compelling and complex main character will be your most difficult job. Secondary characters are more fun, because they can be extreme, quirky, even one-dimensional.

Let's first distinguish between the two. The main character or characters occupy the most space in the novel. That is, more words are written that concern them than concern other characters. Often (though by no means always) they are also the point of view characters.

In other words, he, she or they are the people whom your novel is most *about*.

The secondary characters are the supporting cast. They will take up relatively less space. They may have stories of their own, but at least some of their existence is in the service of the main character(s), either because (1) they help drive the story of the main character(s) forward, and/or because (2) their own stories are thematically linked, and/or (3) they reflect the social milieu of the main character(s).

The main character must change as a result of the plot of the novel. If there is more than one main character, the most important one must change. If the main characters are truly of equal weight, at least one of them must change. This is the minimum—*all* the characters in a novel can change if you want them to.

The majority of novels have a single main character whom we

recognize immediately as the main character. Holden Caulfield is the main character of *Catcher in the Rye*. Scarlett O'Hara is the main character of *Gone With the Wind*. David Copperfield is the main character of the book of the same name.

But sometimes a book stars two (or more) main characters who have equal, or almost equal, weight. In *Anna Karenina* there is a landowner named Konstantin Levin (about whom more later) whose story takes up as many pages as Anna's. Although we might choose Anna as the *main* main character just because of the title, Levin has just about the same importance. In *The Great Gatsby*, Nick Carraway is almost as important as Gatsby; some might argue more so, in spite of the title, because he's the one who tells the story (also, he's the one who really changes; Gatsby dies with his dream intact).

Kate Klimo wrote a book called *Labor Pains* which interweaves the stories of five women as they go through pregnancy and child-birth. Each of the women has about the same amount of time devoted to her. So *Labor Pains* can be said to have five main charac-ters. Going from the popular to the classic, it would be very difficult to say who the single most important character in *War and Peace* is, though I'd probably vote for Pierre.

Just as there is no rule for the number of main characters that a novel can have, there's no limit to the number of secondary charac-ters. Neither are those secondary characters created equal to each other. In *Gone With the Wind*, Melanie, Ashley and Rhett aren't main characters in quite the same way Scarlett is but they're far more important—they're *closer* to being main characters—than Scarlett's sister Suellen. In *Les Miserables*, Jean Valjean is the main character. But Marius, Fantine and Cosette are larger, more important second-ary characters than the rebels or Eponine, the street girl who loves Marius.

The point is that characters in a novel don't line up on two sides of the road under two billboards bearing the signs, Main Characters and Secondary Characters. Rather, characters are on a continuum, with main characters on the order of Scarlett O'Hara, Holden Caul-field and David Copperfield on one end, and characters on the order of the Yankee whom Scarlett shoots, the doctor who attends David Copperfield's birth and the homeless boys of *Les Miserables* on the other. There are many stages in between.

The closer a character is to being a main character, the more complexity, stature and ability to act on a goal that character must have. The smaller the role the character plays in the novel, the more narrowly you can focus on the character's personality.

The Cracked-Open Door

You know many people in your life in a limited way. The clerk at the grocery store whom you see a couple of times a week is only a grocery clerk to you: rude or friendly, efficient or slow. You don't know her as a dedicated volunteer at a crisis hotline or a loving companion to her ailing father.

In the same way, you only know your shrink in the role of shrink, your dentist in the role of dentist; even the main way you know your mother is as your mother.

Since a secondary character is on stage for less time and often exists largely in relation to the main character, creating a secondary character is like looking at a person through a partially open door.

That doesn't mean that a secondary character should be dull. Quite the contrary. Paradoxically, in fact, their very narrowness gives the author an opportunity to examine certain aspects of the human experience more closely.

Take Miss Havisham, from Dickens's *Great Expectations*. She's a secondary character. We know very little about her beyond the fact that she was left at the altar some years ago, only minutes before her wedding. Since then, Miss Havisham has made being jilted into a lifestyle.

When we meet Miss Havisham we see an old woman, sitting in a yellowed wedding dress, shut up in a darkened room with a stopped clock. She's been sitting there for all these years, ever since she got the news that the marriage would not take place.

Dickens's image of the old woman in the wedding gown is a stark picture of bitterness. That's all Miss Havisham is: bitterness and a desire for revenge toward the male sex. But that's all she has to be, because her primary purpose in the novel is to bring Pip and Estella together and to begin the process of Pip resenting his working class background and aspiring to be a gentleman.

Miss Havisham isn't really all that believable, and she certainly isn't complex. But by focusing primarily on that one aspect of her personality, Dickens is able to say, "Look at what happens to a person who lets bitterness rule her life." Miss Havisham literally shrivels up inside her wedding dress.

Now, imagine Miss Havisham as the main character of a novel, *Miss Havisham's Blues*. After the first chapter in which we see her preparing for her ill-fated wedding, the book would bog down. Miss

Havisham doesn't have the complexity required to be a main character. Her bitterness would wear us down. "Get over it, honey," we'd yearn to say, no later than chapter two.

But as a secondary character, we can almost love her, the way you would a *meshuganah* relative whom you went to visit once in a while.

A good, if extreme, example of the narrowness of secondary characters is Disney's version of *Snow White and the Seven Dwarfs*. Snow White is the main character. The dwarfs are secondary characters, with one personality trait each: Doc, Sleepy, Happy, Bashful, Sneezy, Dopey and Grumpy.

I said earlier that a character should not be a mouthpiece for a philosophy, and I meant what I said. But since you can focus more narrowly on your secondary characters, they can sometimes dramatize various points of view more naturally than a main character. For example, in *The Brothers Karamazov*, Dostoyevsky writes of a saintly priest who embodies Christ's teachings, and who serves as an inspiration to young Alyosha Karamazov. Alyosha Karamazov is a main character. He has to struggle to achieve the same level of goodness that Father Zossima possesses, and Alyosha slips up. But as a secondary character, Zossima doesn't need to struggle; he can simply represent an ideal that Dostoyevsky wanted to put forth.

A secondary character can be just plain funny in his extremes. Cliff Claven, the mailman/barfly from the television show *Cheers*, only has a few sides to his personality: he's a middle-aged man who lives with his mother, and hangs out in a bar spouting pompous-sounding but usually incorrect information on subjects nobody cares about.

If Cliff Claven got his own show, if Father Zossima or Miss Havisham got their own novels, they would have to develop a lot more complexity. Cliff would probably need a real love interest. Father Zossima would struggle with temptation. Miss Havisham . . . well, she'd definitely need a life.

But as long as they're secondary characters, keep them in their place.

The Barney Fife Syndrome:
How Secondary Characters Try to Take Over a Book

It's a common pattern in novels that the main character becomes rather dull while the secondary characters are compelling and lively. What happens, I think, is that the author is having so much fun with her quirky secondary characters that she almost unconsciously spends too much time writing about them, while ignoring the star of the show.

Actually you can see this in many successful novels. Charles, the main character of *Brideshead Revisited*, is a pretty dull guy compared to Lord Sebastian and his siblings.

David Copperfield is a solid enough character but not much competition for Mr. Micawber, Uriah Heep and Steerforth.

It happens on television, too. Mary Richards is a serious snooze compared to Ted Baxter, Murray and Mr. Grant.

Charles, David and Mary testify to the strong centrifugal force exerted by secondary characters. But it's all a matter of degree: While both *David Copperfield* and *Brideshead Revisited* are magnificent books (and *The Mary Tyler Moore Show* an excellent program), others may sink beneath publishability because the main character disappears. If you find that your main character is not pulling his weight, then be prepared to dig deeper into him. Make him more complex. Give him more stature. Give him goals he can feel passionately about. Make sure he's getting the page time he deserves. Most importantly, put him back into the center of the action—and then let him *take* action.

Whenever you're having trouble with your characters (main or secondary), don't be afraid to go back and do some of the character-developing exercises listed in this book, or even repeat some that you've done already. Each time you'll discover new aspects of them, build on what you've done.

Making Characters Memorable When You Have to Put Fifty of Them on a Bus in the First Chapter

Any good writer wants to make her characters memorable. What's the point, otherwise?

But novelists, and some novelists in particular, have an extra job to do in this department, just because of the sheer numbers of characters they're juggling. A short story rarely has more than half a dozen characters and even when it has twenty-five, a story's over before the reader can forget who's who.

Some novels, too, are fairly short and sparsely populated (although, in order to *be* a novel, a work must be 50,000 words). So, the question of making characters memorable in a novel such as *The Great Gatsby* is less troublesome than in *Bleak House*. This is not to say that Fitzgerald relied on brevity to make his characters stay in our minds: Jay Gatsby, Daisy and Tom Buchanan, Nick Carraway and Meyer Wolfsheim are some of the most memorable characters in literature and would be if they were part of a two thousand pager.

But if you are writing a long book with a really lot of characters, you do face an additional challenge.

In some genres a *dramatis personae* or family tree is placed at the beginning of the book to help readers keep track. This is most often seen in fantasy or historical novels where characters are many and names are long and unfamiliar, making them even harder to remember. The device isn't limited to these genres, however: some editions place family trees at the beginning of such classics as *War and Peace*, *Wuthering Heights* and *One Hundred Years of Solitude*.

Clearly, though, Tolstoy didn't shrug off his responsibilities as a novelist by saying, "Oh, well, I don't really have to develop Nikolai Rostov as a character, because everyone can just flip back to the beginning to remember who he is."

And you shouldn't, either. The first and best way to make characters memorable is to make them complete, living, breathing characters. Main characters will be more complex, which will make them memorable; secondary characters will be less complex but more extreme, which will make them memorable.

However, there are some additional techniques for dealing with the limits of a reader's memory.

Introduce Characters in Relation to the Main Character

This technique is especially useful when we have to meet several characters close together in time. Let's say you're writing a novel about a young woman named Jane, who moves to Berkeley to attend the university. Your novel will be about how Jane goes to work on the campus newspaper and discovers a scandal in the agriculture department.

In the first chapter, Jane answers an ad for a room to rent in a large house, already occupied by seven semi-weirdos. You write the scene in which she comes over to meet everyone and gain their approval before she moves in.

First she meets Fuchsia, a chain-smoking twenty-year-old with hair the color of her name.

Then she meets Ed, a handsome senior with his own car.

Then she meets Bobi Sue, fresh from her Alabama farm, who wants to major in astronomy.

Then she meets Abdul, an exchange student who wants to become an engineer.

Even with these four characters you probably get the idea; imagine if Jane meets seven or more. Sure, comic possibilities abound, but only if we can remember who we're talking about.

So when Jane meets each one of these roommates-to-be, let her react to them or they to her in such a way that a potential conflict (good) or a full-blown conflict (better) is created.

> Jane looked at the cigarette in Fuchsia's hand. "Is smoking allowed in the house?" she asked.
>
> "In my house it is," Fuchsia replied, exhaling in Jane's face.
>
> "Don't worry about Fuchsia." A young man approached them from the other end of the hall and took Jane's elbow. "She just likes to shock new kids on their first day. We actually make her go outside with that poison."
>
> Jane studied the young man. He had day's growth of beard and a cleft in his chin. What put her over the edge was that she caught the scent of Old Spice, the aftershave her father had always used.
>
> "Hi," he said, holding out his hand. "I'm Ed."
>
> "J-Jane," she stammered, clasping it.
>
> "Don't get excited, Sweetie." Fuchsia dragged on the cigarette. "Our Ed has about three girlfriends already. There's only so much one man can do."

The tension between Jane and Fuchsia and Jane's attraction to Ed will lodge them in our minds. In real life we remember people most vividly in relation to ourselves. Fiction isn't always like real life but in this case it is.

Give Them Stories

We already decided that this novel is primarily about Jane uncovering a scandal in the agriculture department. Her life with her seven roommates may be mostly a densely-populated subplot. Chapters may go by between Fuchsia's and Ed's appearance, which will make them even harder to remember.

What the writer can do is to create ongoing stories for the characters, thus creating suspense about them that keeps them in our minds between visits. For example, when Jane first meets Ed he tells her that his car has been impounded because he hasn't paid five hundred dollars' worth of parking tickets. Next time we see him, Jane asks, "What's happening with your car?" and he gives us an update.

Or Fuchsia admits, after her little tiff with Jane, that she's trying to quit smoking, and every time we see *her* she gives us an update on her battle (not necessarily summarized in dialogue; maybe we see her with a nicotine patch). Ed may get his car back and Fuchsia may quit, but then they'll get into other scrapes.

Obviously, the stories they live will further characterize them. Ed is showing us who is he by letting the tickets pile up on his car, Fuchsia by her desire to shake her habit.

Avoid Laundry List Intros When You Can

Jane doesn't have to meet all her roommates on the same day or in the same scene. An alternative would be to give us the scene in which Ed, as senior member of the house, interviews her and gives her the go-ahead to move in. Later, when she moves in, Fuchsia comes into her room, plunks down on her bed and lights up. And still later, Jane meets the others.

This gives the reader a better chance to become acquainted with each character individually. But even then, you'll want to have conflict in the scenes, because in a novel there's always conflict.

Tag 'Em

Another device for making characters memorable is to tag them with immediately identifiable physical attributes, mannerisms or verbal tics.

We've talked about how gestures, physical appearance and speech reveal character, and the tags that you choose should be significant, not arbitrary. Here, though, the point is also to use these mannerisms, etc., repetitively so that the reader will immediately associate those details with a certain character. "Boyd came in, his sleeve rolled up to reveal the tattoo of the heart with his mother's name on it." If, whenever we see Boyd, we'll see the tattoo of the heart, we start to think, "Oh, Boyd—tattoo. Boyd—tattoo."

You don't see elderly women wearing wedding dresses every day, which is one reason that Miss Havisham is memorable from the first time we see her. Dickens was masterful at tagging characters in this way. Uriah Heep, the conniving clerk from *David Copperfield*, constantly baits the adult David by referring to him as "Master Copperfield," a title then reserved for children. Another character in the same novel, Dora, is always with her little dog.

We'll remember a character who hobbles into a scene on crutches, especially since that character will have to keep fumbling with the crutches as he sits, stands or tries to get something from the refrigerator.

Sometimes the tag almost becomes part of a character's name. I had a friend who briefly wrote for television before becoming an attorney. Although law was more profitable for her, it wasn't such an unusual career and so years later Emily still found that she was regularly introduced at parties as "Emily-who-once-wrote-an-episode-of-*Guiding-Light*."

In *Boys and Girls Together*, William Goldman tagged all his characters with a variety of gestures. One man has an odd way of lighting a cigarette, another of pushing glasses up his nose with his thumb.

These tags work well for fairly minor characters who might otherwise be eclipsed by the characters who appear more often. Very minor characters don't need *that* much characterization, after all; we mostly just need to remember them.

You can definitely use tags for more important characters, too, as William Goldman did. But those characters will need to be more than just a compilation of repetitive gestures; they'll need to be complex. You already know that, though.

Vary the Names

I sometimes see novels-in-progress with important characters named Lisa and Liz, or Stan and Sid. But using names that look or sound too much alike, especially if those characters frequently appear together, makes things needlessly more difficult for the reader. Don't do it unless you have a very good reason.

A student of mine was writing a novel peopled with what another student termed "grunt names:" common, three- and four-letter names like Beth, Ann, Kate, Tom and Bill. Even though the names weren't particularly similar, none stood out, which made the characters hard to keep straight, in spite of their different personalities.

I thought this student was simply missing an opportunity to use rich and varied names both to characterize and to make her characters memorable. You can do this, too. Mix up long and short, unusual and popular. Think about ethnic background. Don't forget what names mean: Amy means "loved;" Peter means "rock." Donna means "lady."

Different names are popular in different generations. My mother's name is Helen, but I don't know anyone under the age of ten with that name. Many women my mother's age were named Shirley, after Shirley Temple. I hope to live to see the time when America is full of Grandma Tiffanys.

My children attended preschool with MacKenna Hernandez, Harrison Goldberg, and Nehemiah Casciato. Their classmates' names reflected both San Francisco's ethnic diversity and two current trends in given names: androgynous surnames-as-first-names and Old Testament prophets.

Sometimes a walk-on in a novel might be identified throughout his or her brief appearance by a striking physical characteristic. The narrator refers to a woman wearing periwinkle eye shadow as Blue Shadow, or to two cops who arrive at the scene of an accident as Big Cop and Little Cop. Here the name becomes a tag.

Sometimes We Don't Have to Remember

Your novel is about a young couple from a small town who move to Manhattan and first become corrupted but then rediscover their values and prevail.

In the opening chapter Young Couple is married in a church in their little hometown in Nebraska. The church is full of all their friends and relatives—two, three hundred people who watched Young Couple grow up.

Young Couple can't wait to ditch this hick burg and split for the Big Apple. But you, as author, want to use this wedding scene as an opportunity to convey to the reader the world that Young Couple is leaving behind.

Go ahead and describe a whole laundry list of the guests. "Abe whose wife was killed in that grain elevator fire, though no one ever quite figured out what she was doing out in the grain elevator at 2 A.M." "Becky Miller, who always wore her hair down to cover her big ears."

We'll need to see a lot of the guests so that we'll share the experience of being present at a big wedding. In this case the guests are almost part of the scenery. We don't have to remember them, if we're not going to see them again, but we will carry away an impression of the lives, loves, hopes and woes of people in this small town.

Don't Give Us More Characters Than We Need

To tell you the truth, the first question I would have asked the author of the novel about Jane and her seven roommates is, "Does she *have* to have seven roommates? Could you combine them, maybe make it five, or even three?"

But the techniques we've discussed will be useful when you do need a lot of characters. After all, what would Snow White have been with only one dwarf?

REWRITING NOTES

Writing the first draft of a novel is like going over Niagara Falls in a barrel. As you huddle in that barrel you are not overly concerned with the form of your plunge—you just want to make to the bottom—and out of the barrel—alive.

Although our focus in this chapter is character, let's talk about rewriting in general for purposes of this entire book. Muddle through your first draft. Make all kinds of mistakes, know that you're making them, but don't worry about them. When it comes to novels, nobody gets it right the first time. You've got to get that first draft written or you'll have nothing to rewrite.

I think it's a good idea to take a week off between finishing the first draft of your novel and starting to rewrite it. Spend the time working on a short story or poem or article you've been thinking about. OK, maybe go to *one* movie.

Then sit down and re-read your first draft straight through. This way you will simulate as closely as possible for yourself the experience of an objective reader.

In the process of writing our minds sometimes fill in gaps that we're leaving on the page. In other words, *I* know that Jasper can't help being unfaithful to his wife Nora, even though he loves her, so I may forget that the reader won't know that unless I include Jasper thinking, *Why am I doing this? I love Nora, not Penelope. But instead I'm hurting both of them—and myself most of all, because if I lose Nora I'll die.* If I don't write that, the reader may see Jasper only as an adulterous louse, instead of a conflicted man.

So when you re-read your novel, imagine that you picked it up in a bookstore, paid $24.95 for it, and brought it home with few if any preconceived notions. Make your mind *tabula rasa*.

As you re-read, make notes about your impressions. *Can we really believe that Mrs. Grimsby would leave her entire fortune to her cat? Can I make Allegra a little less nasty in this chapter?*

Note, *all* your impressions, not just those concerning character. In the area of characterization, however, look not just for the gaps you may have left, but for what you may have overstated. The repetitive mannerism is a good way to tag a character, but if they occur too often they can be distracting.

Very importantly, what have you "told" that you could have "shown"? Is there anything in narration that would be better dramatized? Anything in a scene that isn't really worth a whole scene?

Look carefully in particular for telling words, which were illustrated earlier.

Jot down any ideas you have for rewriting, if they occur to you. But don't stop and rework the novel. It's important to read it straight through in order to get that sense of reading it as an actual reader, rather than as the author.

After you've re-read the novel once and collected your notes, you can do an additional exercise for tracking individual character development. Take an extra copy of the manuscript and go through it, highlighting the dialogue of each important character (the main and the *almost*-main characters at least, but you can do it for more minor characters if you choose). Then go through the manuscript once for each of the characters for whom you've done the exercise, reading only that character's highlighted dialogue. Does a distinct way of speaking emerge? Is the character believable, complex, consistent, yet unpredictable? Dialogue is a good way of honing in on characters because it's the most immediate, the one time the character is speaking directly to the reader.

Characters aren't real people, but like real people they are in a constant state of development. By the time you return to the beginning of your novel, after slogging through a first draft, you will know a lot more about your characters than when you sat down to type "Chapter One." (That's another reason why it's important to take the entire plunge down Niagara Falls before you start fiddling around. When you've written that first draft, you're a novelist, even if the book isn't finished yet. Tinkering around for two years with an opening chapter does not a novelist make, even if those opening pages get to be very polished.)

And keep in mind that the first draft of a novel, especially a first novel, will usually require more than a polish. It will probably need an overhaul. That's often true of second, third and fourth novels, too. You won't save any time by tweaking it here and there, improving sentences and sharpening exchanges of dialogue, when the center will not hold. It's like painting over the dry rot in your house.

As Annie Dillard wrote, in *The Writing Life*, on the subject of hefty rewrites, "That is why so many experienced writers urge young men and women to learn a useful trade."

The work itself is hard, and it's painful to throw out perfectly good material. I have nothing to say about the former, which is simply a true statement. But about the latter I can at least remind you that your work is not part of a limited supply, a vein of gold that will eventually exhaust itself. Writing is more like a skill that, once learned, you can practice indefinitely, just as a surgeon who learns to take out an appendix can do so an unlimited number of times.

At this stage you may want to go back and do more of the character-developing exercises, especially for any characters whom you feel need work. Do this even if you've already re-visited those exercises in the process of writing the first draft. Each time should get you more deeply into the characters, and doing them will be good preparation for the second draft.

Most of the writers I know become very emotionally involved with their characters. I've seen some take it a bit far, like a friend of mine who frequently referred to his main character as his son.

But a few idiosyncrasies are permissible on the part of the writer if the result is a compelling fictional character. I always wondered, in fact, what makes the truly successful fictional characters more interesting than so many real people. When I read this passage in E.M. Forster's *Aspects of the Novel* I found a good answer.

> In daily life we never understand each other, neither complete clairvoyance nor complete confessional exists. We know each other approximately, by external signs, and these serve well enough as a basis for society and even for intimacy. But people in a novel can be understood completely by the reader if the novelist wishes; their inner as well as their outer life can be exposed. And this is why they often seem more definite than characters in history, or even our own friends; we have been told all about them that can be told; even if they are imperfect or unreal they do not contain any secrets, whereas our friends do and must, mutual secrecy being one of the conditions of life upon this globe.

The conditions of life in a novel are happily not so restricted, which makes a novel a good place to go to escape the restrictions that do exist here, especially if we can meet people in that novel who are worth knowing.

Additional Character Exercises:

1. Do this one with a friend, or your writing group. Have everyone take a magazine and cut out a few bodies from various advertisements. Spread them out on a table. Then everyone should choose one magazine-body and write a description—physical, psychological, biographical—of that person.

2. Choose a person from your childhood whom you hated. Maybe it was the fourth grade teacher who humiliated you when she singled you out in front of the class for your poor artwork, or the bully who terrorized you on the playground. Write a sympathetic description of that person. For example, you might describe how that fourth grade teacher was trying to motivate her student to daydream less and apply herself more.

3. Sketch out a description of a character. Then choose a traumatic event or major life change to befall that character—he lives through a 7.1 earthquake, loses a loved one, gets fired and can't find another job. Describe how that character changes.

4. Go back to some of your earlier writing—preferably something from a few years ago, if you've been writing that long. Take one of the characters from that earlier work and make notes to yourself about how you perceived that character. Then put him or her in a brand new scene. Try to find ways to go deeper into that character, and reveal his or her character more effectively than before.

5. Choose as a character an animal, such as a cat, or an inanimate object, such as a coffee table. Put this animal or object into a scene; let it interact with a human or another animal or object. For example, describe how your two cats argue about whether or not you're a good owner, or let your coffee table complain to you about having to bear the weight of all those silly art books. Make your cats and coffee tables quirky.

CHAPTER THREE

A Plot Should Not Be Where the Writer Is Buried

THE BASICS

I've known a few writers who were born with the gift of plotting. Shocking revelations (Adelaida is really the Count's daughter!), reversals of fortune ("All our money was in that diamond mine, Elizabeth") and subtle clues ("Her parasol was wet . . . but it hadn't rained all week") seem to come naturally to them. Either that, or they get visits from the plotting elves.

But those lucky folks notwithstanding, my observation is that, overall, plotting is the single most difficult task a budding novelist faces. For many of us, nothing is more difficult than creating, sustaining and concluding a satisfying plot. You might say that we're plotting disabled, though personally I prefer to be called plot challenged.

Some writers give up early in the battle. They point to some obscure novel completely without a plot, about a man who lives in a studio apartment with a cockatiel. (Never mind that six people read the book, including the author's editor and agent.) They say, "See? Not every novel has a plot. I can get away without one. Plot doesn't interest me."

But plot sure interests readers.

The characters may be what we care about, but the plot is what *makes* us care, because it is through their actions (which in turn drive the plot), that characters reveal themselves.

And, as E.M. Forster said, "Yes—oh, dear, yes—a novel tells a story."

A plotless, or poorly plotted, novel will not only be more difficult to sell, it will be a bad book. And my grandmother would want to know, "Is *that* what you want to write? A bad book?"

That doesn't mean you have to construct an intricate, three-tiered plot with Perils of Pauline-style cliffhangers at the end of each chapter. There are many rooms in the House o' Plots, from Hemingway's fairly simple *The Old Man and the Sea* to John Barth's intricate *The Sot-Weed Factor*.

But something has to happen in a novel, something that holds our interest. A novel isn't about an ordinary day in the life of your character; it's about an *extra*ordinary day, or week or years. That requires some power of invention on your part.

I can't send the plotting elves to your house because, believe me, if I could track them down I'd keep them locked up in my basement. But what we can do in this chapter is break down a plot and see how it works, and then talk about some ways that you can start putting together your own.

Story vs. Plot: A Definition

The terms "story" and "plot" are often used interchangeably, and often they can be. However, a plot is something more than a story.

According to E.M. Forster (in *Aspects of the Novel*), story is "a narrative of events arranged in their time sequence." The King died. The Queen died. The prince raised taxes. That's a story.

Forster continues, "Plot is also a narrative of events, the emphasis falling on causality. 'The King died, and then the Queen died of grief,' is a plot."

And then the prince raised taxes because he needed more money to support his mistress.

This may suffice to define plot, but it doesn't define a *good* plot. For that, I'm going to give you my own definition, because it's my book. *A plot is a series of causally related events that emerge from a series of ever-intensifying conflicts and prove a premise at the end.*

Literary vs. Popular Novels
(and the Reason Both Need Good Plots)

Plot gets a bum rap in some circles. We associate the well-plotted novel with the thick paperbacks gleaming in racks in airport newsstands, the kind of book you'd kindly leave on the seat for the next passenger when you disembark in Denver.

Some of my students share this disdain. They're bright and educated and they want to be real artists, even though they've been warned about the pay and the hours. They're among the ones I told you about, who tell me they want to write novels about characters.

But in fact, a good novel about characters does have a plot, it just comes about differently.

Let's take popular novels first. Back in the 1970s, a physician named Robin Cook wrote the definitive medical thriller, *Coma*. Here is the plot, in simplified form: Susan Wheeler is a blond, blue-green-eyed, voluptuous, young medical student. On her first day making hospital rounds, she sees a woman her own age—twenty-three—who has gone into a coma. No one can give Susan a satisfactory explanation of what caused the coma. Susan begins poking around and asking questions.

She collects evidence and formulates different theories but only toward the end of the novel—after visiting an institution where comatose patients are in effect warehoused, and overhearing a key conversation—does she figure out that a group of evil doctors are slipping carbon monoxide into certain patients' oxygen during surgery. As a result the patient loses cognitive functions but remains technically alive so that his or her organs can be sold to wealthy people who can not only afford to buy such amenities, they can even buy livers that match the upholstery in their Rolls Royces.

Coma is a darn good book of its type. It's a well-plotted thriller; it preys on everyone's fear of hospitals and surgery; and by looking at ethical breaches in the extreme, it raises the very real ethical questions that doctors face every day. Who should get priority for scarce available organs? How long should a body without hope of regaining cognitive functions be kept alive at great expense?

It's also clear that the plot is primary. Cook *starts out* with the conspiracy. That's what's important. Susan Wheeler is the perfect heroine to solve the mystery. She has stature: she's sexy and at the top of her medical school class. (This is what feminism has done for us so far: Now you have to be both smart *and* big-busted.) She's complex: feisty, soft, determined, seductive. But she serves the plot, not the other way around. Cook developed her character to go in and solve the mystery. He doesn't deliver any particular insight, for example, into why someone becomes a doctor, why a woman becomes a doctor or how working with ill people holds a mirror up to one's own mortality.

At the other end of the spectrum are the literary novels. Anne Tyler's *The Accidental Tourist* is such a book.

Macon Leary is the main character. His last name reveals that he is leery of life and all the risks it presents. He is complex, and he has stature (he's the successful author of travel guides), but he does not have the ability to act upon a strong goal, which actually makes him more difficult to care about until the end when he finally begins to get some intestinal fortitude.

Macon's wife, Sarah, has become tired of Macon's rigidity and idiosyncrasies. Just before the book begins, Sarah and Macon's only son is murdered, and that tragedy becomes the catalyst that forces her to leave him.

Macon almost "accidentally" becomes involved with a young woman named Muriel, who with her flamboyant appearance, lack of education and erratic temperament is far removed from Sarah. Macon and Muriel seem ill-suited and when Sarah seeks a reconciliation it seems at first that Macon, who's taken so little responsibility for his life, will rush back to the security and familiarity she represents. But he chooses to stay with Muriel.

There's plenty of plot in *The Accidental Tourist*: an off-scene murder, the Learys' separation, the subplot of an unlikely romance involving Macon's sister. But it's quite obvious that the author's mission is to explore the nuances of the personalities of Macon, Sarah and Muriel, and how those nuances affect their destinies. *Character is primary.* The plot flows from the nature of the characters: Sarah's grief causes her to leave Macon; Macon's passivity prevents him from keeping her; Muriel's determination wins Macon. When Macon decides to stay with Muriel after all, it's because he realizes, "His marriage, his two jobs, his time with Muriel, his return to Sarah—all seemed to have simply befallen him. He couldn't think of a single major act he'd managed of his own accord. Was it too late to begin now?" Such a subtle reflection would be lost in a book like *Coma*.

If you glance down the *New York Times* best-seller list, you will definitely see more popular novels than literary novels on an average day. But literary novels can land there (Anne Tyler's have) while many popular novels languish on bookstore shelves, or worse, in warehouses. What makes a novel literary or popular isn't how many copies it sells (most writers write in the hope that their novels will sell well), but rather just the distinction between plot and character that we've been discussing. You may also note that literary novels rely on a more original use of language, whereas popular novels tend to be more accessible, to reach the broadest popular audience.

I believe that a good popular novel is just as difficult to write as a good literary one. *Coma* is a good popular novel. Robin Cook proceeded to write some bad ones after that, repeating his own formula without the originality. *The Accidental Tourist* is a good literary novel. I won't name any bad ones, but there are plenty.

Each type of book demands different skills. If you set out to write a popular novel write the very best one you can because, believe me, there's plenty of competition. Writing a popular novel is no excuse to ignore character any more than writing a literary novel is an excuse to ignore plot.

The Building Blocks of Plot—Conflict

Let's break down plot into its smallest element and build an entire plot from there.

Just as a foot is comprised of inches, so is a plot comprised of conflicts. Conflicts themselves can be broken down like this:

A character wants something.

But he can't have it, because of an obstacle.

That character now has a conflict.

If the obstacle he faces is in the environment or embodied in another character, the conflict is external.

If the obstacle is within the character himself, the conflict is internal.

Examples:

• A woman wants to travel to Europe. She can't because she doesn't have enough money. This is an obstacle in the environment, and she has an external conflict.

• A different woman wants to travel to Europe, but *she* can't because her boyfriend is jealous and doesn't want her to go. There the obstacle is embodied in another person and is again external.

• A third woman wants to travel to Europe, but doesn't go because she's afraid both of flying and seasickness, and there's no way to get to Europe without flying on a plane or sailing on a ship. This obstacle is within herself and she has an internal conflict.

Building a Plot From Conflict

Once the author has put her character in conflict, the next step is that the character take action in order to resolve the conflict, that is, to overcome the obstacle and get what he wants. (Sometimes the character is acted upon, but it is preferable that the character, especially the main character, himself take action.)

When the character takes action to resolve the conflict he will either resolve the conflict while creating a new one in the process, or intensify the original conflict, or both.

Examples:
These three illustrations take the example of the second woman who wants to travel to Europe, the one with the jealous boyfriend.

• The woman argues with her boyfriend over her planned trip to Europe. He refuses to see things her way and finally in disgust she ends their relationship. Thus, *old conflict resolved, new conflict created.* She's removed her obstacle to traveling to Europe. But in the process she'll create a new conflict—or at least she should, in order for the plot to continue. In this case, perhaps, she'll arrive in Europe wanting to find a new boyfriend, and the obstacle will be internal: no man seems to qualify when she compares him to her old flame, even though he was so unreasonable on the travel issue.

• The woman argues with her boyfriend, insisting he let her go on this trip. He refuses to see things her way. The woman is left exhausted and angry from their argument, but she still wants to go. *Same conflict, now intensified.* The woman has taken the most immediate and obvious action; now she'll have to dig deeper into herself to come up with something more drastic. (This is one of the places in which plot and character meet; the events of the plot themselves give the author an opportunity to reveal the character.)

• The woman argues with her boyfriend. He still refuses to let her go. In fact, he says, he's been seeing another woman, and if First Woman insists on taking this stupid European trip, he will end their relationship for good and take up with the other woman permanently.

The woman presumably still wants to go to Europe but now not only is the obstacle greater, but she has a new conflict: she wants her boyfriend to stop seeing the other woman; he doesn't want to. *The original conflict is intensified and a new one created.*

All three of these scenarios end with a character in conflict. So, once again, the character takes action (looks for a new boyfriend, books a flight to Paris), and once again finds herself in conflict (either the old one intensified, or a new one, or both). And so the process is repeated until the novel reaches its conclusion.

The Most Compelling Conflicts

You will describe many conflicts in the course of a novel, some banal, some profound. But here let's note that the most compelling conflicts, the ones that form the spine of good books, will be conflicts in which both parties are right, or at least have a good case to state.

- In *Anna Karenina*, although we side with warmhearted Anna against rigid Karenin, Tolstoy often lets us feel the difficulty of the betrayed husband's position. Karenin's done nothing particularly wrong, but he's being publicly humiliated by his wife and her lover.
- In *Les Misérables*, Jean Valjean is a fugitive from "justice." (This is one of the truly great novels. The musical is also one of the truly great musicals, but as a writer, you should definitely read the book as well.) Valjean was originally imprisoned for stealing a loaf of bread for his sister's starving family, and because of two escape attempts, he served nineteen years in prison. In spite of the unbearable harshness of his life, after he's finally released, he's redeemed and goes on to live a righteous, almost saintly life. However, there's the small matter of his having committed a misdemeanor while on parole and he is being pursued by Inspector Javert, a detective who has vowed to track him down.

Like Alexey Karenin, Javert is a man who sees justice as what's written in the law, not what's felt in the heart. He's cast as one of the villains of the book (though there are others more truly villainous). But in Javert's head we understand his point of view. To him, Valjean is an incorrigible criminal, and justice must be done.

You can probably see that complex characterization more naturally makes for compelling conflicts. Alexey Karenin is more than a rigid prig. Inspector Javert is more than a RoboCop.

Some genres demand more thorough-going villains and even in literary novels, some conflicts will be pretty one-sided. But be very wary of writing about characters who are always victims of cruel society, fate or ex-husbands. When you can present two sides of a case, you make your novel soar.

But What's the Point?—The Premise of *Cinderella*

A series of conflicts strung together is necessary but not sufficient for a good plot. Those conflicts must also be selected and ordered in a way that gives the plot meaning. This meaning is embodied in the premise.

Let's first look at how conflicts are strung together in the story of *Cinderella*, which will then serve to illustrate the concept of premise. *Cinderella* is an old tale with many versions; mine is a slightly shortened telling from the Brothers Grimm.

After giving us some background about Cinderella's blended family, the story introduces its first conflict. Cinderella wants to go to the ball, but she faces an obstacle: She doesn't have a thing to wear. This is an external conflict, personified by Cinderella's stepmother, who could give her a dress if she wanted.

Cinderella takes action to get what she wants by beseeching her stepmother to take her to the ball along with her stepsisters. Her stepmother responds by taking a shovelful of linseed and throwing it into the hearth. She tells Cinderella that if she can pick them out within an hour she can go to the ball.

Cinderella takes action: She calls upon the local birds, who throughout the story act as messengers of Cinderella's dead mother, and who are well-equipped for the job. They pick the linseed out.

But when Cinderella goes to her stepmother with the recovered linseed, Stepmom laughs, "Ha, ha, ha! That was just a joke, Cinderella! You didn't really think I was going to take you to the ball, did you?"

Off go Stepmom and Stepsisters to the ball, *sans* Cinderella, who remains at home with the same conflict (she wants to go to the ball; she faces an obstacle). But now the conflict is intensified. Cinderella has tried to get what she wants. She's begged; she's called in a favor with her bird friends. She's done her best. Now she must dig deeper into herself, come up with something better.

And she does. Once again, Cinderella takes action. She goes out in back of the cottage where her mother is buried. There a tree has grown from her mother's grave where Cinderella's tears have fallen. From that tree, after Cinderella sheds a few more tears, a lovely ballgown falls.

Cinderella wears it to the ball.

Now the first conflict is resolved: She's at the ball, no more ball to want, forget the ball. But immediately a new conflict is created. The prince sees Cinderella, dances with her and wants to know who she is so he can make her his bride. Cinderella wants to hide her identity, presumably because she feels unworthy, being a scullery maid by day and all.

Cinderella takes action to get what she wants (which is to hide her identity): She runs away without telling the prince where she's going. She returns home where she leaves her ballgown on her mother's grave.

In the Grimms' version there are three balls and the process is repeated at the second one. But by the third ball the prince has gotten wise: He spreads pitch on the steps of the palace to trap Cinderella. (Taking action, you see, to get what he wants.) Cinderella slips on her way out and one of her shoes gets stuck in the pitch. She still manages to escape, but the shoe is left behind.

The prince still wants the same thing—to discover Cinderella's identity—but the conflict has been intensified. The prince has just gone through what Cinderella went through with her stepmother. He went to the limit and found it wasn't good enough. So now he has to dig deeper into himself, to find resources he didn't even know he had. Once again, the plot is forcing a character to become more than he already is. The week before the prince probably would have said, "Hey, they *all* want to marry me. Why should I put myself out?"

But here comes Cinderella, so beautiful and pious that the prince is willing to hit every single home in the kingdom to find her. Even with a small kingdom that's got to take a while.

So the prince sends a messenger to go door-to-door to find the woman whose foot fits in the shoe.

When the messenger arrives at Cinderella's house we have at least two conflicts going on at once (often this will be the case). Cinderella's stepmother wants the prince to marry one of *her* daughters. She faces an obstacle in Cinderella, whose foot is more likely to fit the shoe. Her action to get what she wants is to shut Cinderella away in the kitchen.

The first stepsister tries the shoe on in another room, but it doesn't fit. The stepmother offers her a knife with which to cut off her toe. ("When you are a queen," she cogently observes in the original Grimms' fairytale, "you will not want to use your feet much.")

With the first stepsister ensconced in the shoe, the messenger thinks he's got his gal, and rides away with her. But as they pass by the grave of Cinderella's mother, one of the birds calls out from the tree, "Yoo hoo, Messenger Boy! Catch the blood on the flank of your white charger?"

The messenger brings the first stepsister back. Same conflict; parties more desperate. Stepmother produces second stepsister, this time persuading the girl to cut off her heel in order to wear the shoe, under the same forceful argument that swayed her sister. And once again a bird calls it to the messenger's attention. Little slow, that messenger, but I guess that's why he's just a messenger.

Back at Cinderella's house, the story reaches its climatic scene. The messenger demands to know if there are any other maidens in the household. Stepmother protests that there is not. The messenger knows his job is at stake; the stepmother would rather croak than see Cinderella get the guy. But finally Cinderella is brought out from the kitchen.

She tries on the shoe; the rest is herstory.

Epilogue: At Cinderella's wedding, her bird friends once again appear, this time to peck out her stepsisters' eyes.

The story of *Cinderella* has gripped us for centuries in its many different forms. (Not long ago, Colleen McCullough retold it in a novel called *The Ladies of Missalonghi*). Why is it so phenomenally durable?

Because the point of the story, the conclusion we reach at the end, is that "beauty and goodness triumph over evil and ugliness." All the conflicts of the story lead up to proving that.

This point, this conclusion, is the *premise* of a story.

Every good novel, short story or screenplay will have a clear premise that the events of that novel prove at the end.

The Premise as Change in Character

A well-proved premise will be another link between plot and character, because the premise, besides being the conclusion we draw at the end of the plot, will also be a restatement of the most important change that the main character or characters goes through, or the lesson he or she learns.

The premise of *Pride and Prejudice* is "women will find the husbands they deserve." Elizabeth Bennet, kind and clever, with reason to believe that she would become an old maid, instead ends up the wife of a really rich guy.

The premise of *Bonfire of the Vanities* is "oppression practiced by a class will be avenged on an individual." Sherman McCoy goes from self-described "master of the universe" to professional scapegoat, bearing the rage of the African-American community.

The premise of *Peter Pan* is "people grow up, but the spirit of youth never dies." Wendy returns home to grow up but she'll always remember Neverland.

The premise of the movie *Star Wars* is "goodness triumphs over evil." The characters in *Stars Wars* are fairly simple, but Luke Skywalker discovers his ability to tap into the Force and fight for good. He goes from being space farm boy to staturesque good guy; he triumphs over evil.

(Remember that the main character or characters of a novel must always change as a result of the plot. Secondary characters may or may not.)

The purpose of the premise is not necessarily to preach a lesson, since really good fiction contains at least some ambiguity as to who's right and who's wrong. The premise as you prove it will grow out of the characters. In *Madame Bovary*, Emma Bovary commits adultery and it leads to her death. But that's because that's who Emma is: so heedless of consequences that she borrows money on all her and her husband's worldly possessions to support her grand illusion of a great love until, facing ruin and with no way out, she swallows poison.

This is true in pop as well as literary fiction. In *Coma* it is Susan Wheeler's intrepid sleuthing that allows Cook to prove the premise that *illegal activities lead to being caught.*

Other Elements of the Premise

One Premise per Novel

A good novel is rich in incident and open to many interpretations. You might look at *Cinderella* and say, "Who does Prince Charmwhoever think he is? Choosing a bride from all the maidens of the kingdom. Huh. Seems to me that another premise of *Cinderella* is that 'absolute power corrupts absolutely.' "

But if that were the premise, then it would be better proved if the prince decided to choose two or three wives. Only one premise can be solidly proved.

Even in a novel with several subplots, this is true, and we'll illustrate how in the section to follow on subplots.

A Premise Need Not Be Universally True

Does beauty and goodness always triumph over evil and ugliness? Don't make me laugh, OK? And as for the premise of *Anna Karenina*—"adultery leads to death"—I can think of at least two or three people who have proved otherwise.

A premise needs to be universally true within the novel itself. But Tolstoy could have written another novel later in which he proved the premise, *adultery leads to a happy life*, if he'd wanted.

A Premise Can Be Re-Used

The story must be original, and your writing must be as well, but a good premise never wears out. We've already seen that *Anna Karenina* and *Madame Bovary* have the same premise, although they're very different books.

In fact, there are probably no more than three premises to describe 90 percent of all the films produced by major Hollywood studios:

Love conquers all.

The little guy can beat the big guy, if he tries real hard.

Goodness triumphs over evil.

You can write more than one novel with the same premise, or write a novel that has the same premise as a previously published work of fiction.

A Premise Must be Specific

There are many ways to prove any premise, but a premise such as "Life is hard" is so vague that it doesn't provide any guideline. You could apply that premise to any story that doesn't end happily, just as any story that *does* end happily could theoretically have the premise "Life is good."

To make sure your premise is specific enough, make sure that it has two parts. That is, one condition leads to another, or is compared to another, or is qualified in a definite way, as in:

- Being good leads to being taken advantage of
- Love requires compromise if it's going to last
- Evil is always punished
- Greed leads to success

A Profound Premise Does Not Make a Profound Book

Theoretically a premise-*qua*-premise may be quite trivial. But if you develop characters well inside a conflict-driven plot, you will almost inevitably prove an interesting premise.

You set out to write a novel with the premise, "Los Angeles is a better place to live than San Francisco." (You'd be wrong, of course, but we've already said that a premise need only be true in the context of the novel.) You show us a young man who travels first to San Francisco but who finds the people so politically correct that they're ultimately incapable of real feeling. The young man journeys to Los Angeles where ambitions and prejudices alike are on the surface. He finds the atmosphere more honest.

So although you have on one level told us that Los Angeles is a better place to live, you have really proved something about people: "It's better to be honest about your feelings than to try to pretend those feelings are nobler than they really are."

Similarly, choosing a grand premise will not ensure that your novel is equally grand. The premise of *The Bridges of Madison County* is that "great love lasts forever," but that book is no *Romeo and Juliet*, which has a similar premise ("Great love defies even death," according to Lajos Egri in *The Art of Dramatic Writing*).

The Purpose (for the Writer) of a Premise

A reader will love to read a book that has a well-proved and interesting premise. But articulating a premise for yourself has a benefit for you as a writer, as well. Your premise is like a cat's whiskers.

A cat has whiskers that are exactly as wide as the widest part of its body. That way a cat can tell whether or not it can fit in the gap in the picket fence, or the cat door you sawed last weekend. If its whiskers brush up against the side of the door, it knows not to try to go through.

Similarly, you can hold your premise up to your plot and ask, does this scene contribute to the premise I want to prove?

If not, you can get rid of it.

There's no scene in *Cinderella* in which the King and the Prince discuss the recent crop failure, because it wouldn't further Cinderella on her inexorable journey from scullery maid to princess.

Everything in *Anna Karenina* leads to the moment in which Anna's adultery ends in her death. From the time she first meets Vronsky and senses his attraction to her, she's on the slippery slope. That's why there are no chapters about her childhood as a circus performer.

If you know the premise of your novel before you start writing your novel, *mazel tov*. But if you don't, please don't worry. I believe that you should write a first draft without being overly concerned about the premise. If you start with too rigid an idea about premise or any other element, you may lock yourself into a plan that doesn't work and miss opportunities to tap into deeper levels of your own talent.

However, once the first draft is complete, decide what the premise is, then brutally hold it up to your novel to see whether you've proved it or not. Then ask yourself, what can I cut, add or alter in order to prove it better?

Upping the Stakes

Another aspect of a good plot, complementary to what we've already discussed, is that the stakes increase from beginning to end.

First, it's important that throughout a novel we know what the stakes are. By stakes, I mean the importance of the outcome of the events to the characters. Without knowing that, how can we care about what happens?

If I'm a billionaire, and I buy a lottery ticket that might win me another five or so million dollars, my stakes in the outcome of the lottery are low. But if I'm a poor woman who's taken in laundry all her life and who now desperately wants to send her beloved son to medical school, winning the lottery may be my only hope. The stakes for me in that case are much higher.

But whatever the stakes are at the beginning, they should keep going up. What this often means is that the incidents of a novel become gradually more dramatic. A conflict surrounding a first date in the first chapter becomes a conflict surrounding a wedding in the second, a birth in the third, a divorce in the fourth.

But you don't have to go from burnt toast in the first chapter to nuclear fallout in the last. What you do need to do is show us how *the investment of the characters in the outcome of the conflicts is continually greater.*

Cinderella begins with Cinderella wanting to go to the ball. We care about that on her behalf, because we can see the poor kid deserves to go to a ball. What's at stake is a night on the town.

At the ball the Prince falls in love with Cinderella and wants to discover her identity. If he does, he'll make her a princess. So now what's at stake is Cinderella's entire future.

Imagine if instead, Cinderella went home after the balls and started dreaming about next year's balls. On its face, it would be harder for us to care about her going back next year because we've already seen her accomplish that goal.

In Scott Turow's novel *Presumed Innocent*, a deputy district attorney named Carolyn Polhemus is murdered. Another deputy D.A., Rusty Sabich, is investigating her death. Rusty had an affair with Carolyn, so what's at stake is both his reputation and his desire to know what happened to a woman he lusted for deeply, if didn't exactly love.

But then Rusty is himself arrested and charged with the crime. Now what's at stake is his freedom. (Turow cleverly weaves in a description of the horrific prison life of a white collar criminal so we know just what Rusty faces if he goes to jail; this is a way of making the stakes clear.)

Imagine *Presumed Innocent* in reverse. Rusty Sabich is charged with the murder of Carolyn Polhemus. He valiantly defends himself with the help of his attorney, Sandy Stern. After he's acquitted, he goes to seek her real murderer. On its face, it's not as exciting. But again, the stakes are upped because of the investment of the characters in the outcome of the events, not because of the events themselves. Therefore, *Presumed Innocent* could in fact work in reverse if, for example, Carolyn were the one true love of Rusty's life, and his concern about avenging her death was actually greater than his concern for his own life.

How It Works

As a fairly subtle example of how the stakes can be raised as a book progresses, let's look at Fannie Flagg's novel, *Fried Green Tomatoes at the Whistle Stop Café*. (I remember Fannie Flagg from the old *Candid Camera* show, which makes me older than I ever thought I'd be.)

Fried Green Tomatoes at the Whistle-Stop Café is a fine book, which also makes use of an ambitious structure: a story unfolding in the past and a story unfolding in the present, the former affecting the latter. There are many characters, but the ones who concern us here are Idgie (short for Imogen), Ruth, and Ruth's husband, Frank.

Idgie is an independent-minded woman who loves Ruth, but Ruth marries a slimy character named Frank. Idgie tries to resign herself, but when she learns that Frank is beating Ruth she comes and takes Ruth away. The two women live together happily. One day Frank comes looking for Ruth, to reclaim her. Later—much later—his body turns up in the river.

Idgie is tried for the murder. Many years have passed and Ruth has died of cancer. Idgie is acquitted, because the parson gallantly lies to cover for her—gallantly because Idgie has never been a friend of the church.

Fried Green Tomatoes at the Whistle-Stop Café was made into a movie, called *Fried Green Tomatoes*. Movie adaptations often disappoint the serious fans of a book, since many nuances and often as many characters and subplots are lost. Some memorable people dropped out of *Fried Green Tomatoes*.

However it came about, though, the film version made one improvement over the book: When Idgie is tried for murder, Ruth is still alive. This makes the stakes of the trial much higher: If Idgie goes to jail (or hangs), it will be a loss for Ruth as well as for Idgie. Not to mention that Idgie will lose not only her freedom, but her relationship with Ruth.

And when Ruth dies of cancer shortly thereafter, Idgie's trial and acquittal makes Ruth's death even more poignant: Here Idgie has triumphed over the obstacle of Frank, only to lose Ruth anyway. Compared to the film version, Idgie's trial after Ruth's death in the book is somewhat anticlimactic. Although Idgie is hardly the kind of woman to give up on living no matter what happens to her, once she's lost Ruth she doesn't have as much at stake in the outcome of the trial.

How Character Can Do the Job

Plot and character once again meet in the area of increasing stakes because, to some extent, if you are developing your characters well, digging ever deeper into the complexities of their personalities, we as readers will naturally become more invested in what happens to them, and the stakes will rise because of our increasing interest.

But don't take that for granted. You should of course be developing your characters well under any circumstances. Make sure that the story is gaining momentum, too.

And a very important caution: Don't hold back at the beginning of your novel on the theory that, if the stakes must continually increase, you must start at a low point. Start at a high point and go to ever higher points.

How the Heck Do You DO It?

Several pages ago you may have become a bit disgruntled, thinking, "Well, I just love to hear about all these elements of plot, but it doesn't do *me* any good. I still need Plotting Elves."

Be sure and call me if they show up at your house. Meanwhile, there will be a great deal of trial and error for those of us who are plotting disabled. But I do have a few suggestions for starting to put together your own plots, and here they are.

Strengthening Your Plotting Muscles

Look for opportunities to practice coming up with story and plot ideas, the same way you make a habit of observing people in order to develop the skill of characterizing.

• Go to a museum that displays at least some representational art. Spend the afternoon going from painting to painting and making up stories about the people in them. How do the daughters of Edward Boit in the John Singer Sargent painting feel about each other? Who is that man sitting in the café in Van Gogh's *Café Terrace at Night*? Is he being blackmailed by his mistress over the money he owes?

• At the end of the day (but at some point before you get too exhausted to think), try to remember those fleeting fantasies. *Gee, that plumber sure is cute. Maybe I could drain my credit cards of their cash advances and run away with him.* Or maybe you saw a billboard for a vocational training school and for half a second you imagined chucking your job as a grade school teacher so that you could become a computer programmer.

Write a half-page synopsis of a novel in which someone lives out these fantasies.

If you tend to think in disasters, you can use that, too. What if the car that ran the stop sign *had* smashed into you? Or the furtive-looking man ahead of you in the line at the bank had pulled a gun on the teller?

• Do a detailed outline of a favorite book or movie. This can be time consuming and tedious but well worth the effort. Examine each scene to identify the conflicts. Look at how each character takes action to get what he or she wants, creating new conflicts and intensifying old ones.

• When you finish reading a book, ask yourself, how would I have improved the plot? Maybe gotten the main characters together sooner, or put them under more pressure, forcing them to take more action?

Pick up the threads of the story fifty pages before the end and jot down an alternate ending.

Brainstorm

This is the sometimes frustrating, sometimes fun and most commonly used method.

In your own novel, ask yourself, what happens next? and then set yourself the goal of writing down ten possibilities. The goal in brainstorming is quantity, not quality, because once you start thinking in terms of quality you start censoring your ideas, which entirely defeats the purpose of brainstorming.

When you brainstorm you hope that ideas will lead to other ideas. You can't get to the good idea until you record a couple dozen bad ideas, which might lead you by association to the good ones.

So let go. Be stupid.

Anna and Vronsky join the Hare Krishnas . . .

Anna and Vronsky open a piroshki stand . . .

Anna and Vronsky move to Italy . . .

You have to surrender to a process that may or may not lead anywhere. Usually it will, if you're patient. Make it fun, anyway. Try writing down ideas on index cards or small strips of paper. Shuffle them around or pin them on a bulletin board where you can change the order.

Work Backward

This is brainstorming in reverse. Some writers find it helpful to start with their desired ending and back up from there. This is almost crucial in a mystery, but it can work in any type of plot.

You know that in the end it will turn out that Cornelius murdered the Duke by beating him to death with his polo mallet. Well, what would Cornelius have done with the bloody mallet? Maybe he buried it in the woods. Maybe the Duke's bloodhound can dig it up. So that gives you an idea for a scene in which Lady Elaine and Hollingsworth are walking in the woods with the dog and the dog starts sniffing excitedly. . . .

Or you're writing a romance. You know that you want your couple to end up together after many trials and tribulations. What's the worst tribulation you can think of? A flame from the past? An IRS audit? After you've chosen the disaster, you can back up another step to see what causes it.

Reversals

A staple of plots is the "reversal of the situation," as Aristotle called it. One day, Oedipus is a mighty king; the next, he's a blind committer of incest.

Twenty years ago I was hanging off the side of my bed reading *War and Peace*, when I got to the part when we discover that Prince Andrei, whom we thought was dead, is alive. I'll never forget the moment. This is a reversal: We thought he was dead, but he's alive.

So when you brainstorm, ask yourself, how can you take your characters from high positions to low positions, low to high?

Think of the Reader

Ask yourself, if I were the reader, what would satisfy me? Given these characters, what would I like to see happen to them? Don't worry about pleasing the reader by giving her exactly what she wants, but be sure you *interest* her.

Borrow

You can borrow plots. Shakespeare did it, so it must be OK. He did it so well that people borrow from him: *Romeo and Juliet* into *West Side Story*, *King Lear* into Jane Smiley's *A Thousand Acres*.

There's an old saying, "Good writers borrow; great writers steal." It's actually a joke. You can't and wouldn't want to steal someone else's plot. But what you can do is look to other authors' work for inspiration. If you loved John Irving's *The World According to Garp*, you can challenge yourself to invent the same type of bizarre-yet-somehow-believable events in your own novel. If you're moved by *Anna Karenina*, you might ask yourself, what would happen if a woman like Anna, living in modern Manhattan and married to a city councilman, met a dashing young stockbroker. . . .

Go Back to the Characters

Whenever you're stuck, *go back to what the characters want.* This is especially important in a literary novel. But even if you are writing a book like *Coma* you can use it. Susan Wheeler wants to figure out why so many patients have become comatose at Boston Memorial hospital. What will she try next to further her investigation?

Let Your Research Give You Ideas

You're writing a novel about a ranch foreman, but you've never lived on a ranch. (I have to ask, then why are you giving yourself such a headache, writing about a ranch?—but I guess it's none of my business.)

So you go and live on a ranch for six months. You already have an idea for the novel itself: It will be about the unlikely romance between the ranch foreman and a small-time country-western singer who comes through town.

Talking to real ranch foremen, and real country-western singers, will be extremely important if you want to come up with the authentic details that will make the events of your novel believable. But in the process you may also get ideas for the plot. Suppose a ranch hand tells you the local legend of the ghost who haunts the abandoned stables and comes out whenever the wind is blowing east. . . .

A scene in my novel *California Street* took place in a county jail. I'd never been to the county jail, I'm happy to say, but through a friend I was able to arrange a visit. The deputy sheriff who took me around told me the story of a man confined there who, in attempt to get transferred to the psych ward, tried to eat his jeans, starting at the waist. I wasn't able to use it in the plot per se, but I did throw it in as a detail.

Your background reading may give you ideas, too. Researching the Tudor monarchs you learn of the little-known story of Margaret Kentworth, a lady-in-waiting who spoke out against the practice of blood-letting and who was tried for heresy.

Plot Patience

In the early stages of writing your novel, there will almost inevitably be gaps in your own plotting logic. But we novelists must put a lot of faith in our unconscious minds to provide us with the raw material; then we must use our conscious minds, and elbow grease, to shape that raw material into something fine.

It's hard. Believe me, I know it's hard. But with patience you can do it.

THE FINER POINTS

Subplots

Like a plot, a subplot is a sequence of casually related events. What makes a plot a subplot is first of all that it occupies less space in the novel, but also that it is in some way *sub*servient to the main plot. It either refines the premise of the book, drives the main plot forward, or at the very least, provides us with a context for that main plot. It might even accomplish all three.

Even the shortest and slightest novel will have at least one subplot. Otherwise you will have written a long short story. The necessity of subplotting is one reason writers find novels so intimidating, and it's also one reason that sometimes writers who have mastered the short story have a tough time making the transition to novels. Some short story writers think that all they have to do is keep the short story going for three hundred pages, instead of stopping after twenty, and they'll have a novel. Not so. A novel is not only longer than a short story, it's wider.

Most novels will have a distinct main plot and one or more subplots. But sometimes a novel will have two or more main plots of equal weight. A book like that may or may not have other subplots in addition.

But whether you are dealing with a plot and a subplot, or two main plots, the various events can't just be arbitrary, other-things-that-happen to flesh out the book. They are part of the composition of a novel which, once complete, seems so effortless and whole, and they have to be connected in some way.

And a well-structured novel, no matter how many plots and subplots it has, will prove one premise.

Let's look at the three main types of subplots and how they ultimately fulfill this goal.

The Plot-Linked Subplot

The most challenging and intricate subplots are those that drive the main plot forward.

As an example, let's look at one of the emblematic books of the 1980s, Tom Wolfe's *The Bonfire of the Vanities*. *Bonfire* tells the story of Sherman McCoy, an arrogant bond trader whose life unravels after he and his mistress get lost in the Bronx, and run over a young black man. The hit-and-run accident becomes a *cause célèbre* for the entire city of New York, a symbol of racial oppression; ironically, in the end, Sherman's punishment isn't to go to jail but to get stuck in a kind of criminal justice system limbo in which he must defend himself forever.

Sherman McCoy is an interesting case of a hero who evolves into an anti-hero. He's pretty unlikable, and he's quite a bumbler, too, as his getting lost in the Bronx reflects. But he has stature, as the scion of an upper-class family and a wealthy bond trader. And he's complex: Although snobbish, he's capable of real feeling for his daughter, his wife and, of course, his girlfriend.

So, at the beginning of the book, when society is on Sherman's side, he qualifies as a hero. When society turns against him to drag him down, he becomes an anti-hero. Ironically, his fall is what redeems him as a character because although Sherman is kind of a jerk, he doesn't deserve to have his entire life destroyed. After all, he's not solely responsible for the social injustice that is revenged upon him personally; he's being used as a scapegoat, so that the injustice can continue.

The two main subplots of *Bonfire* (there are several, more incidental subplots as well) concern, first of all, Larry Kramer, an assistant district attorney who is looking for a Great White Defendant to bolster his career, and secondly, Peter Fallow, an alcoholic British journalist who must find a good story to cover for similar reasons. Wolfe creates complex lives for both Larry Kramer and Peter Fallow, but for each of them, the central goal becomes to nail Sherman, the perpetrator of the hit-and-run. Therefore, as each character either comes closer to or is pushed farther away from his goal, Sherman is affected, and thus Sherman's story moves forward even when he's off-scene.

This makes for an admirably dense novel, because the same phenomenon works in reverse: when we read about Sherman we are also reading about Larry Kramer and Peter Fallow, because the outcome of Sherman's story—whether or not he achieves *his* goal of escaping the consequences of his involvement in the hit-and-run accident—affects them as well.

The Premise-Bound Subplot

It's always satisfying for us as readers to see subplots that intersect with main plots. It appeals to our wish to see life itself make sense and, although we don't want to see coincidences that stretch our credulity, we like to see an author's godlike skill at tying various threads together.

But for a subplot to function, it is not absolutely necessary for it to intersect with the main plot, if it serves to prove the premise.

Once again, *Anna Karenina* can serve as an example. We've already summarized the main plot of the novel, which describes how Anna Karenina meets Vronsky, has an affair with him and ends her life. I mentioned in chapter two that there is another character in *Anna Karenina* who takes up as much or even more page time, and whose story is probably of equal weight to Anna's. He is the gentleman farmer Konstantin Levin.

We actually meet Levin before we meet Anna. Levin has arrived in Moscow to propose to the beautiful young Kitty Shcherbatsky. Like everyone in the novel, Levin is an extremely complex character: dour and socially awkward, but practical, hard-working and highly sensitive.

Levin has had reason to hope that Kitty might accept him, but when he arrives on the scene at the beginning of the novel she has been receiving the attentions of none other than Count Vronsky himself. Kitty refuses Levin's proposal, which he takes as final. Shortly thereafter, Vronsky abandons his courtship of Kitty (which he himself had never taken very seriously) to devote himself to his pursuit of Anna.

However, some time later, Levin and Kitty come together again. They marry and have a child, and suffer some rather typical trials and tribulations of the first year of marriage, a sort of Russian *Barefoot in the Park*. They fight over little things, and reconcile over big things. The love of his wife and child make Levin a stronger yet gentler man, and toward the end of the book, Levin, who has been an agnostic up until now, experiences a religious conversion. His soul is saved.

The characters in Anna's story and the characters in Levin's story overlap—Kitty's sister is Anna's sister-in-law—but the overlap is quite incidental. The two plots do not drive each other forward the way that Peter Fallow's and Larry Kramer's stories drive Sherman McCoy in *Bonfire*. However, they are linked by the premise. We already know that the premise of Anna's story is that *adultery leads to death*. And now we can see that the premise of Levin's story, the conclusion we reach from the events depicted, is that *fidelity* (or, a happy family life) *leads to salvation*. The two premises prove each other.

When the subplots, or other main plots, of a novel are separate in this fashion, then they must be bound by the premise, otherwise they will seem arbitrary, like stories that belong in other books.

In chapter two I also mentioned a book by Kate Klimo called

Labor Pains. The novel follows five women through their experiences of conception, pregnancy and childbirth. The women all meet in a Lamaze class, and two of the women know each other from outside the class, but for the most part they live their lives entirely independently from each other. Klimo tells their stories in continuing drama fashion. The book is divided into several parts—conception, first trimester, etc.—and in each of these parts a section is devoted to each character.

Each of the women live in the New York area and each represent a different item on the zeitgeist checklist. One is an older career woman who has fertility problems. One is a single woman who decides to have a baby on her own. One is a married woman having an affair who is unsure whether her husband or her lover has fathered her child.

Labor Pains is definitely pop fiction: The characters have been plugged into this template of contemporary issues. Even when they give birth they all undergo something that would come out of a woman's magazine article entitled, "The Childbirth Experience." One woman has natural childbirth. One woman has a Caesarean. You get it.

But, although the content of their personal lives vary, at the end of the book each woman has proved the same premise: *The joys of motherhood are worth the sacrifices.* At the end, each woman either has a baby or is expecting a baby (one woman miscarried, but became pregnant again), and each has learned that whatever compromises in love or career they've had to make, babies are what it's about. Although you can probably infer from my summary that I'm not bowled over either by the writing or the characterizations of the book, the structure of *Labor Pains* is quite sound.

Labor Pains gives roughly equal weight to each of five women, but this premise-bound structure works the same way with subplots that are clearly of less importance.

Let's say that you want to write a searingly insightful young-people-adrift-in-the-big-city book. You assemble a group of various types who all move to San Francisco: a shrewd entrepreneur, a promising artist and a lawyer who wants to help the poor.

You decide to make the artist your main character and to focus primarily on her story as she struggles with the temptation to paint trite, tourist-pleasing city scenes instead of the more challenging canvases she sees in her mind. In the end she refuses a fairly cushy job as an illustrator with an advertising agency and decides to seal herself in her room to paint.

The artist shares the same Victorian flat with the other two important characters, but their interaction is limited to waiting for each other to get out of the shower. Still, you want to spin out a couple of subplots and the artist's roommates are the most natural candidates to be the stars of those subplots.

It will be important that the premise of those subplots support, or perhaps refine, the premise of the main plot. Maybe both the entrepreneur who wants to open a catering business and the lawyer who wants to help the poor will similarly struggle with compromising their values. Perhaps they'll hold onto their ideals, perhaps they'll sell out. What matters is that at the end we can draw *one conclusion* from all three tales. In this case it might be, *only the strong survive the pressures of the big city.*

Through your subplots you can make your premise very complex. Let's say that your artist-main character is a temperamental, self-torturing genius. In the end, she decides to paint, to be a true "artist." But her lawyer roommate decides that helping the poor doesn't pay well enough, while the entrepreneur decides that she'd rather work for a large restaurant than try to run her own business. Here the premise might be, *only people with true genius can stay true to their dreams.* The plot and subplots will elucidate how the lawyer and the entrepreneur don't quite have what it takes, but the artist does. (Once again, plot and character meet.)

It's still one premise, and that's all that matters.

Subplots can *both* refine the premise and drive the main plot forward. In this last example, it might turn out that it is the lawyer who helps the artist break her contract with the ad agency. Maybe the entrepreneur offers to help the artist financially. Or perhaps the painter, the lawyer and entrepreneur all fall in love with the same man.

The Subplot as Social Context

The setting of a novel—its time and place—is always crucial in terms of providing a context for the behavior of the characters. The setting can inspire one or more subplots as well.

Don't get me wrong. When I hear writers say, "The Grand Seto Bridge has become a character in my book," I disagree. Bridges, cities and other elements of a setting can't be characters, because they have no wills of their own. They don't want anything and if they change it's because the people around them cause them to change. Cities, mountains or lakes may be symbols; they may help create or heighten a mood. But they're not characters.

Similarly, the setting of a novel in itself is neither plot nor subplot. But when people take action to cause the setting to evolve,
or when the setting of the novel forces them to take action, *that's*
a plot (or subplot). That plot or subplot may either drive the main
plot forward or refine the premise, or both. But even if it just provides context for the actions of the main characters, by virtue of
establishing the social and/or political milieu, it makes more sweeping statements about what has shaped the people of this time and
place, and even what might affect them in the future.

Historical novels often provide the most obvious examples of
settings that inspire subplots. Take *Gone With the Wind*: The Civil
War and Reconstruction are subplots of the novel. The people of
the South want to secede and the people of the North don't want
them to; that's a conflict. Each side takes action to get what it wants,
by killing members of the other side. When the South surrenders
because it's out of supplies and running low on soldiers, a new
conflict is created: The South wants to prosper again but the North
wants to punish the South economically.

The historical subplot drives Scarlett's main plot forward at many
key points. The advent of the Civil War is how Scarlett justifies a
hasty marriage to Charles Hamilton. Later, when Sherman's army
comes upon Atlanta, Scarlett and Melanie must flee on the very
day that Melanie gives birth.

Because the subplot drives the main plot forward it does not
have to prove or refine the premise. You might say that the premise
of the events of the Civil War is that *the better-equipped army wins the
war*. (Rhett Butler in fact quotes Napoleon as making a similar
observation.) However, you can see how the events of the subplot
contribute to Margaret Mitchell proving the premise of the book,
*A woman without values can survive social upheaval, but only at the cost
of love*.

In most historical novels, historical events affect the lives of the
invented characters. Heck, if that wasn't the case, why not just set
your novel entirely in the Mall of America in 1996? What would be
the point if, in *A Tale of Two Cities*, Charles Darnay and Lucie
Manette just stayed home and shook their heads about all that
madness going on in France?

But a subplot can also work primarily as context, in either a
historical or modern novel. Some of the more minor subplots of *The
Bonfire of the Vanities* illustrate this principle. For example, early in
the novel, a man named Edward Fiske III, who represents a church
group, goes to see a certain Reverend Bacon. Fiske is trying to

ascertain what happened to the $350,000 that the church gave the Reverend for a day care center. The Reverend, in turn, subtly threatens Fiske, implying that he can, if he wants, create unrest and even violence in the black community, and that even if he can't account for the $350,000, it isn't much to pay for peaceful neighborhoods. The conflict between Fiske and Reverend Bacon forms a complete, if small, subplot: Fiske is worried about what will happen to his job if he can't recover the money, while the Reverend has every intention of keeping it. That's a conflict, and both characters are taking action to get what they want. But the reason this subplot truly functions is that it provides a context for the main story line: The background it gives us about poverty in Harlem and the Bronx helps to explain, in part, how it is that when Sherman is inadvertently responsible for running over a young black man, he unleashes so much rage.

Foreshadowing

Foreshadowing is anything in a novel that prepares us for something to follow.

Foreshadowing can be quite blatant. Suppose you're writing about a young man being arrested for drunk driving, and in the middle of the scene you tell us, "Twenty-five years later, when he was President of the United States, Bill looked back on this night and laughed."

Paradoxically, such blatant foreshadowing can create a lot of suspense. We'll be quite curious to see how ne'er-do-well Bill becomes President in twenty-five years.

Another type of foreshadowing is more subtle. We think we're just reading the book. But description, dialogue, a character's gesture—anything can contain foreshadowing. We don't necessarily know, as we read the description, dialogue or gestures, that the author is preparing us for future events, although sometimes we may sense that something's afoot, in the emphasis that the author gives a particular detail or passage. Either way, when the later events do occur, we realize that we knew they were coming all along.

As an example of subtle foreshadowing, let's look at this passage from *The Great Gatsby*:

> About halfway between West Egg and New York the motor road hastily joins the railroad and runs beside it for a quarter of a mile, so as to shrink away from a certain desolate

area of land. This is a valley of ashes—a fantastic farm where ashes grow like wheat into ridges and hills and grotesque gardens; where ashes take the forms of houses and chimneys and rising smoke and, finally, with a transcendent effort, of men who move dimly and already crumbling through the powdery air. Occasionally a line of gray cars crawls along an invisible track, gives out a ghastly creak, and comes to rest, and immediately the ash-gray men swarm up with leaden spades and stir up an impenetrable cloud, which screens their obscure operations from your sight.

But above the gray land and the spasms of bleak dust which drift endlessly over it, you perceive, after a moment, the eyes of Dr. T.J. Eckleburg. The eyes of Dr. T.J. Eckleburg are blue and gigantic—their retinas are one yard high. They look out of no face but, instead, from a pair of enormous yellow spectacles which pass over a non-existent nose. Evidently some wild wag of an oculist set them there to fatten his practice in the borough of Queens, and then sank down himself to eternal blindness, or forgot them and moved away. But his eyes, dimmed a little by many paintless days under sun and rain, brood on over the solemn dumping ground.

The valley of ashes is bounded on one side by a small foul river, and, when the drawbridge is up to let barges through, the passengers on waiting trains can stare at the dismal scene for as long as half an hour. . . .

This is a famous passage that deserves close study. As we read it we see first of all that it is simple description. It sets the scene, allows us to see the action. As the book progresses, we can also see how certain thematic notes are struck, which this passage either introduces or reintroduces: for example, the corruption of the American dream, and the replacement of a spiritual god with a material one.

The passage is also laden with images of death. The name Fitzgerald gives to the area he describes—the valley of ashes—evokes both the phrase from the Twenty-First Psalm, "the valley of the shadow of death," and the funereal prayer, "ashes to ashes, dust to dust." The ash-gray men are like ghosts. And even the "small, foul river" evokes the Styx of Greek mythology, the river over which the dead crossed into Hades. These images foreshadow Myrtle's death, which will take place in this very spot, as well as Gatsby's, which while it occurs elsewhere, flows directly from Myrtle's.

Whether blatant or subtle, foreshadowing itself can perform any or all of three functions:

Preparing the Reader for Future Events and Making Even the Most Bizarre Happenings Believable

When you write a novel you create a universe that may have many similarities to our own, but in fact is not our own. The old dictum has it that readers willingly suspend disbelief when they pick up a novel, but actually they suspend it somewhat grudgingly. Whenever you push the reader's credulity, whenever you write something that seems patently "made up," you tick the reader off. "Here I gave this guy a chance to entertain and enlighten me, and now he's asking me to believe in something so lame." Most readers don't let you tick them off more than once.

However, that doesn't mean that you have to write about purely realistic events. Sure, if you did that, your readers might believe in your world, but they'd be less likely to be interested in it. Not to mention the hardship this would create for science fiction writers.

Your job as a novelist isn't to be purely realistic; it's to put down your own odd version of reality, or even your wildest fantasies, and *make* it believable. In part you do that through the authority of your voice as a writer, and in part you do that through the selection of specific details that put us in the scene. If you describe something vividly enough, readers will believe it the same way they'd believe anything they experienced for themselves.

You can also make your world believable through foreshadowing.

A friend of mine was writing a well-paced novel in which, during the grand finale, an earthquake occurred to further shake up, excuse the pun, all the characters who were already in dire straits. While dramatic, it seemed too coincidental, too *easy*, that an earthquake would occur at that precise moment.

However, all the writer had to do, when she went back to do a rewrite, was to foreshadow the incident. For example, a foreshock of the big quake could occur earlier. That smaller quake should have an effect on the characters, too, but if a quake occurs at a time that isn't for the author's convenience, then it establishes that this is a place where quakes occur, and when one does occur for the author's convenience, the reader will buy it.

It is also good, although not necessary, that foreshadowing not only prepare us for future events but function in the present of the story.

When we first meet Anna in *Anna Karenina* she is arriving in Moscow to help repair the faltering marriage of her brother and sister-in-law. She has shared a compartment with a certain Countess Vronsky, whose son, Count Vronsky, comes to meet her. Thus Anna and Vronsky meet.

Moments later Anna, Vronsky and the others hear that a guard has been killed by a train that ran over him. The tragedy is compounded when they learn that the dead man also was the sole support of a large family. Anna is distressed. Vronksy disappears, and when he returns we find out that he has given 200 rubles to the widow. Thus the incident becomes a way to demonstrate Vronsky's immediate attraction to Anna; he clearly makes this gesture to please her.

But it is a good example of foreshadowing as well because, as you know, Anna herself will die when she throws herself in front of a train. What the incident does for us is to establish that in nineteenth-century Russia, people die from having trains run over them. The scene plants the knowledge in our minds, perhaps unconsciously. When Anna dies this way, it seems less melodramatic or convenient, more destined. This is how foreshadowing can prevent the reader from feeling that you've used something as a device.

Creating Suspense

Often writers think that they can create suspense by withholding information, but in fact the opposite is the case. Imagine a scene in which a woman awakens very early because she's worried. She's too worried to go back to sleep, so she goes down to the kitchen to make coffee. She drinks it. But she's too worried to really enjoy it, so she goes to take a shower.

The writer of this scene may think that she's creating suspense by withholding the cause of this woman's worry, but you can see just by reading this description that we quickly lose patience. We're being *told* that the woman is worried, but not given enough specifics either to believe it or to care. In this atmosphere, the banal details of her life become, if possible, even more banal.

But imagine that same woman rising early in the morning and thinking, *Today is the biopsy. I wonder what they'll find.* It is the paradox of suspense that the more the reader knows the more the reader wants to know. (And suddenly, we'll find ourselves gripped by those same day-in-the-life details.)

You can also create suspense by foreshadowing. The most obvious way is with blatant foreshadowing, as in our earlier example.

"Twenty-five years later when he was President of the United States, Bill looked back on this night and laughed." If the author tells us this in the middle of a scene in which a young man is being arrested for drunk driving, then the reader is going to be very curious about how the young man is going to turn his life around (or cover up his drinking problem).

More subtle foreshadowing can create suspense, too. The passage I quoted at length from *The Great Gatsby* illustrates this. Just the fact that an author is spending a long time describing a particular location or person signals to the reader that the location or person will be important in the story (upon which promise the writer had better deliver). We begin to wonder, what will happen in this place? Or, how will this person be important? More subtle foreshadowing creates more subtle suspense. A first-time reader of *The Great Gatsby* might not consciously register each image of death. But he'll be intrigued by the description, and it will remain in his mind.

Imposing Unity

A novel may be more or less lifelike, but it's not life. When you sit down to write a novel you are taking life and making it orderly.

An example of foreshadowing that imposes unity comes from a novel that a student of mine was working on. The novel centers around two young women, former high school chums, who are reunited after several years. One of the women is actually in love with the other, although reluctant to tell her. Their relationship as we see it in the novel is a touching mix of adult sexuality and childish affection.

At one point, at a party, the two step out on a balcony. Reminiscing, they disagree over who taught whom to whistle. Then they start whistling a tune from school days. Without discussion, it becomes a competition to see who can hold the final note the longest.

It's an overdetermined moment. (By overdetermined I mean that it has more than one reason to be.) The competition reveals their characters, and how much of their relationship is rooted in their shared youth. But it also potentially foreshadows the turn their relationship will take, and we might infer that the winner of the whistling contest will also be winner at the game of love.

Final Words on Foreshadowing

Let the notion of foreshadowing help you brainstorm your plot. As you read what you've written so far, ask yourself what you may have unconsciously foreshadowed for your readers. In this way, the manuscript may suggest to you future events.

Also remember that readers are pretty smart. They know what goes into a good story. So be careful that you deliver the story you foreshadow. A woman is sitting at her desk paying her bills. She sees that her auto (or health, or homeowners) insurance policy has just lapsed—she forgot to send in the premium. She quickly writes a check and puts it in the mail. In real life, the odds are very high that her insurance will be reinstated without a hitch. In fiction, she's due for an accident (or an illness, or a fire) before the check reaches the insurance company.

Drama

The Ascendancy of Scene

In chapter two we made the distinction between narration and scene for the purpose of talking about character. Now let's discuss it in terms of plot.

Overall, novels have become more scenic over the past hundred years. This is probably due to the influence of television and film, which latter medium has been around for nearly a century already. We've gotten used to *picturing* things.

Although novels have always invited us to picture things, too, they also have their deepest roots in storytelling, an oral tradition. When you have to tell your whole story verbally, you tend to compress. Your listeners have to hold all the important information in their heads. Telling a story is closer to narration; acting it out, as in a play, is closer to scene.

Plays have actually been around a lot longer than novels, but movies and television are so widely available that they are the forms that have really altered the novel. There's nothing wrong with that. Nothing exists in isolation. When photography became available, it relieved painters from the need to paint realistically.

That's not to say that you should write a book that imitates a TV movie-of-the-week. As Annie Dillard said, in *The Writing Life*, "The printed word cannot compete with the movies on their ground, and should not. . . . Novels written with film contracts in mind have a faint but unmistakable, and ruinous, odor."

More than teleplays, and more than most films, novels give the writer a chance to comment profoundly both on the human personality and on society at large. Films certainly have that same potential, but they're much more a vehicle for a director than for a writer. Also, because a film usually has to reach many more people to justify its being, the reality is that they stick more with superficial and commercial material. (Yes, there are exceptions.)

But whatever their limits, the influence of film on the novel hasn't been all bad. To the extent that it causes the modern novel to go from scene to scene, it's positive. If you find yourself writing long passages of pure background, or describing habitual events, you may have a plot in trouble. Make something important happen, and make it happen in a scene.

Just as scenes are the most effective way to characterize, so are they the best way in which to move the plot forward. As the saying goes, we'll believe it when we see it.

Sometimes writers try to avoid scenes that seem too difficult to write. A wedding or a riot, because there will be so many people to keep track of. A rape, because the subject matter is so distasteful. But if a scene belongs in your novel, it belongs, and the reader will feel cheated if it isn't there. Go ahead and write the scene as best you can. If it's beyond your level of skill, writing it is how you will increase your level of skill.

Look at where you cut off the scenes you are writing. Can you take them a little further? Try writing another page. You can always throw it away tomorrow; even if you do throw it away, you'll probably learn more about the characters.

Notice when you decide to get up from your desk. Before you do, push yourself to write two more paragraphs—even if your mom is screaming at you from the next room.

Is This Scene Really Necessary?

The principle that the important events of your novel should be dramatized also works in reverse: You don't want to make a scene out of something that doesn't deserve it. Ideally, each scene in a novel moves the story forward; at the same time it reveals something new about the characters.

Let's say you have a character who is a shoplifter. You dramatize for us the first time he gives in to his compulsion. We see him struggle against it but finally succumb: He sneaks the electric can opener under his parka then leaves the store with much fear, and a tiny bit of hope, that he'll be caught.

Your shoplifter may commit the crime several times before either he's caught or decides to seek help. But each time you write about his shoplifting, you want to be certain that the scene sheds different light on the character and his dilemma, increasing the stakes and moving the plot forward.

Sometimes this is a difficult judgment to make. To help us, I make the distinction between "facts" and "information." Facts, according to Webster's Dictionary, are anything that's true, anything that happens. The shoplifter takes an electric can opener or a magazine or a box of chocolate-covered peanuts. He takes them from Kmart or Payless or Pete's Variety Store. Those are facts.

Information (again according to Webster's) is "knowledge, intelligence, news." It gives us something *more* than facts; it allows us to draw inferences from those facts. Each scene must always give us not only new facts but new information.

The first time the shoplifter commits the crime is hard for him. The second time is easy. You're giving us new information, telling us that at least in this character's case, committing crimes gets easier. New information will allow you to move the story forward because the change in the characters will cause them to act differently. In this case, discovering that shoplifting is easy may cause the character to do so much more frequently, or perhaps to commit other crimes.

But whenever you find yourself covering the same emotional territory in a scene, giving us new facts *without* new information, then you have three choices: Either skip the scene entirely, condense it to narration, or find a way to make it function better (you might accomplish this last by forwarding a subplot or foreshadowing later events, among other possibilities). Which of the three choices you make will depend on the book.

Combining Narration and Scene

Although a good novel generally goes from scene to scene, you could not write novels of much scope without narration, which allows you to cover a lot of ground quickly. You can also combine narration and scene to cover that same ground while keeping the material more dramatic than pure narration would be.

So, for example:

> After stealing the screwdriver from Kmart, each time Jason stole got a little easier. He kept to small objects for awhile—pens, candy, a watch. Then he began to smuggle out larger and larger items: bottles of cold medicine, a notebook.
>
> Once he almost got caught. A young salesgirl, with black hair pulled back in a green ribbon, came chasing after him. "Sir? Sir? What's the bulge in your coat?"
>
> "My cat," he said quickly. "I'm taking him to the vet. You don't want me to take him out of my coat," he added quickly. "He might be contagious."

The salesgirl stepped back and said nothing more.

It should have scared him off, but instead it made him more daring. He tried on clothes and then snuck them out of the dressing room. At the grocery store he loaded the pockets of his denim jacket with apples and grapes.

His roommates sometimes wondered aloud where he got the money for the new CD player and the cellular phone, but Jason merely smiled and said, "I guess my parents are feeling generous these days."

This passage combines narration and scene. It compresses time, but then occasionally stops to describe—more briefly than the usual scene—specific events. It uses the methods of scene-setting to bring some of the narration to life. Using this technique, you can give the reader a lot of narration without boring her with long passages of pure narration.

Memorable Scenes

Everyone who ever read *The World According to Garp* remembers the scene in which Jenny Garp becomes pregnant by copulating with a dying man. Everyone remembers Scarlett's desperate buggy ride out of Atlanta. Everyone remembers Jean Valjean escaping into the sewers of Paris.

In real life, we spend an awful lot of time sitting behind desks, watching TV, talking on the phone, or having meals in restaurants. It may seem natural when writing your novel to go from scene to scene describing such ordinary events. Yes, a couple discussing their relationship over fried eggs at Denny's is a scene. But it isn't, on its face, a terribly memorable one.

Granted, some writers are able to take you to Denny's for fried eggs in a way you've never been taken before. Literary writers in particular have the job of closely observing commonplace transactions. And any good writer should be able to make us see ourselves in others' ordinary lives.

But even short of inventing a new sexual perversion or bringing in an invading army, remember that there's nothing quite like getting people into unusual, stressful, frightening, never-before-happened situations. Get them to the zoo. Screeching monkeys make for good sound effects. Let your characters get drunk and go swimming in the fountain in front of the Plaza Hotel.

My former writing teacher, Leonard Bishop, used to tell us, "Whenever you've got people in a car, and the scene gets boring, have someone find a snake in the back seat."

I think he was kidding, but the principle is sound. *Just make something happen.*

The Elements of a Good Ending

Every author's favorite two words must be "the end." But if you've done your job right, the reader will be disappointed to see the pages dwindling as he nears completion of your book.

Many writers begin a novel with its end clearly in mind. Sometimes as they write they reconsider their original ending. Either way, the two magic words can seem like an oasis to an author who is crawling across the desert of novel-writing. Once that end is in view, the author gets a spurt of energy, and crawls a little faster.

An impatient author might end his book too soon, cutting it off at a dramatic high point without giving us a chance to absorb the shock. *Coma* ends this way. Susan Wheeler has been drugged and taken to the sinister operating room 8, where she is receiving a dose of soon-to-be lethal carbon monoxide. Suddenly the flow of the poisonous gas stops. The police come in, their uniforms peeking through their scrubs. Dr. Stark, the evil physician, knows that the jig is up. *Bam*, the end. Even though this is a plot-driven, rather than a character-driven novel, we would still like a chance to see Susan and Mark (her lover) together, perhaps to learn how Susan's attitude towards medicine and the medical establishment has changed as a result of her experiences, or to hear Susan and Mark make wedding plans.

Even if you find yourself feeling impatient to finish your book, don't rush completion. Each part of your novel deserves equal attention. You want the reader to close the book wishing it weren't over, and yet satisfied that it reached its perfect ending-place. That same reader will eagerly anticipate your next book.

Here are some other factors to consider concerning the end of your novel:

Resolve the Core Conflict

The core conflict is the conflict implied by the premise. In *Cinderella*, the premise is *beauty and goodness triumph over evil and ugliness.* Therefore the core conflict is between beauty and goodness, as represented by Cinderella, and evil and ugliness, as represented by her stepmother and stepsisters.

The premise of *Anna Karenina* is *adultery leads to death.* Therefore the core conflict is between adultery (Anna and Vronksy's affair) and the social and internal forces that ultimately drive Anna to commit suicide.

You must resolve the core conflict, otherwise your premise will remain unproved. If the story of *Cinderella* ended before the messenger demanded to see the third sister, we'd be left with, *beauty and goodness* do something *with evil and ugliness, but it's your guess what.*

Beyond resolving the core conflict, it's up to you how much is left ambiguous. Inevitably, something will be, because it would be too cumbersome to sum up the remaining histories of every single character left alive at the end of a novel.

Traditional nineteenth century novels tied up what loose ends they could. In a typical Dickens epic (excluding, of course, the unfinished *Mystery of Edwin Drood*), everyone's second cousin turns out to be someone else's long lost brother. No romance or financial crisis is left unresolved. The last chapter of George Eliot's *Middlemarch* is called "Finale" and describes the salient details of the remainder of a dozen or more characters' lives. Nathaniel Hawthorne's *The Scarlet Letter* doesn't end simply with Dimmesdale's death, but sketches the rest of Hester Prynne's life and lets us know what happened to the other important characters, Roger Chillingworth and Hester's daughter, Pearl, although he preserves some ambiguity about the latter.

Authors with literary aspirations often seek to create ambiguity in their work. This is a noble ambition. But here we must make the distinction between "rich" ambiguity and purely "confusing" ambiguity. Recall our earlier example, in the section on foreshadowing, of the woman who goes through her morning routine worried, without telling us what she's worried about. That's just confusing ambiguity, because it doesn't give us enough information to make any interesting speculations of our own. When, instead, you make the characters come to life and show us enough about the lives they lead, you can cause the reader to have very strong, but also very different, opinions about them.

I remember leaving the theater after seeing *Annie Hall* with a friend. I was ruminating on the film, too impressed to speak for a moment. *Poor Alvy Singer*, I thought. *So sensitive, so intelligent, that no one can really appreciate him, not even the woman he loves.* Just then my friend observed, "What a sad story. Alvy Singer's so immature, that even when Annie Hall outgrows him he can't change."

This is rich ambiguity.

Whether you explicitly tie up every loose end or not, the information you have given us in the novel itself should allow us to infer a lot about what happens afterwards, even if reasonable readers might disagree on exactly what.

For example, at the end of *The Great Gatsby* we don't know precisely what will happen to Daisy, Tom, Jordan or even Nick (besides that he's returning to the Midwest). But their characters have been so fully revealed by the plot, and they are so rooted in their time and place, that we can easily imagine their futures; we have more than adequate information to do so. The fact that you and I might imagine different futures for them makes for a rich ambiguity that some authors prefer to create, rather than to sum up what happened to everyone involved.

Epilogue vs. Final Chapter

Sometimes an author calls his last chapter the epilogue. This is appropriate where:

1. The events of the last chapter take place some time after the events of the penultimate chapter, which is usually the real climax of the book.

2. The last chapter involves characters we haven't seen before, or who have been minor players in the book until now. These won't be creatures from Mars: they'll be people upon whom the events of the book are having an effect, such as the children of the main characters.

3. There was a prologue which acted as a framing device—for example, Boy Scouts telling scary stories around a campfire. In that case, the novel we read is presumably one of the stories being told and at the end of the novel we might return to the campfire to see what effect the story had on the youths.

Happily Ever After—Sometimes

Happy endings are generally more commercial than unhappy ones. And not just happy endings, but endings in which justice is meted out. Not only does boy get girl, but the embezzler goes to jail, the pious go to heaven, and the loose woman finds herself unable to bear children (and probably forced into prostitution in the bargain).

Many men's and women's magazines and publishers of hardcore genre fiction (the kind published as mass-market paperback originals) literally require such endings for publication. Clearly, much of television and film requires it as well. This is an area where films have been, I think, a bad influence: We're so used to seeing everything work out, no matter how big a reach it is, that we can hardly accept any variation. When they actually hanged Richard Gere at the end of *Sommersby*, I was in shock for a week.

But events don't always resolve themselves happily in life and it doesn't always have to be that way in fiction. What really matters is not that your ending conform to a Hollywood version of morality but that it's consistent with your premise. That is, if your premise is that *a life of crime leads to degradation*, there won't be career criminals in your novel who end up living happily in the suburbs, driving Volvos.

In *Crimes and Misdemeanors*, Woody Allen carefully builds to an end that is disturbing and yet satisfying in its mimicry of real life: A once-good man gets away with murder, the truly good man goes blind, the man who preached faith commits suicide, and the shallow man—instead of the intelligent, sensitive one—gets the girl.

Hopefully, things aren't *that* bad. And granted, part of the power of Allen's ending comes from the fact that films are seldom so downbeat. But I still like to think that novelists have a responsibility to examine the moral ramifications of their plots. Just what are you saying about human nature and the way we prosper or suffer for our actions? Let the ending reflect your view of the world even while you're desperately trying to figure out how to resolve all the subplots without having to kill everyone off in a plane crash.

Coincidence—Sometimes

Depending on the genre, you can use coincidence to a greater or lesser degree. In a comic novel such as Voltaire's *Candide*, coincidence rules. We expect it—and the more bizarre the better. In a more realistic novel, you will use it less or, at least, in a different fashion. In Thomas Hardy's novels there are a number of coincidental meetings, but his form is primarily realistic and none of these coincidences are too farfetched. It probably wouldn't fly if it turned out that Vronsky was really Anna Karenina's illegitimate half-brother, once abandoned on the streets of St. Petersburg, although it would cast an even more evil shadow over their affair.

Some great literature is full of nearly unbelievable coincidences. I mean, what really are the odds that Gavroche would find his own brothers in the streets of Paris (in *Les Misérables*), or that Mr. Micawber should happen by when David is visiting the Heeps (in *David Copperfield*)? In those books, the authors establish early on that theirs is a world in which coincidence occurs to a degree much greater than in real life. In fact, some degree of coincidence greater than life is pretty much a requirement of imposing unity on your fiction.

However, although you have some leeway in using coincidence to *further* the plot, you may not use it to *conclude* it. Let's say that in your novel, a woman is having financial difficulties, when it turns out that the elderly man who lives in the apartment above her, and to whom she's been taking soup, is her long-lost, and very rich, uncle. In one day she goes from being a struggling seller of Mary Kay cosmetics to being a woman of leisure, who can contemplate buying a yacht and touring the Greek islands.

In the beginning or the middle of your novel, that device might work just fine. It will be interesting to see how that dramatic change in lifestyle changes your character.

But the old man-revealed-as-uncle routine probably wouldn't work to conclude the novel. Earlier, solving the character's problem for her will create more conflicts which she can then resolve. But as an ending, the coincidence would not only seem too great, it would cheat the reader out of a chance to see the character grow by taking action of her own.

We can qualify this rule: If adequately foreshadowed, a coincidence *might* cease to seem so coincidental that it just might work as an ending. In the case of the woman having financial difficulties, the author could prepare us in advance for the revelation of the old man's true identity. Maybe she's the last to know. And maybe this is a world in which such revelations are common.

But be judicious. The best endings are earned by the characters, not bestowed by fate.

And a novel must never, ever end, "She woke up to discover it had all been a dream."

REWRITING NOTES

First, Some Sympathy

The end of the first draft is a turning point in the life of a novel. I believe that you should let it all hang out in that first draft—head down blind alleys, take the characters for a day at the beach, riff on any subject that interests you. When it's time to begin the second draft, you must change from improvisational actor to vindictive schoolmarm. Toss out paragraphs, whole scenes, whole chapters that don't work. Kill off characters. Hold the premise up to what you've done and see what crawls through and what doesn't make it.

Unfortunately, this will make for some work.

You've crafted a moving novel about a young man's experiences in the Civil Rights movement in Alabama in the early 1960s. But your writing group persuades you that the plot is thin; perhaps a love interest for the young man will bulk it up while revealing different sides of the character (yet again, plot and character meet).

You can't just write a few romantic scenes and then insert them. The new subplot will ripple through the entire novel. The young man will have his lady friend on his mind at many different junctures. It will affect his behavior, which will in turn affect the behavior of others. The lady friend will herself take action that affects the young man and other characters.

Perhaps you decide that this new character should be not just a passive love interest but a dedicated civil rights worker as well. That might mean that several perfectly good scenes in which the civil rights workers plan strategies or stage protests have to be completely gutted in order to work this new character in.

This is why writers can be very skittish about making changes in their plots. Any rewrites that you do affect the whole, but plot does so the most radically. Ironically, the better the novel, the more interwoven the incidents will be, and the more shaking up you'll have to do on a rewrite.

You have to be brave. If something doesn't work, it doesn't work. Tear it down and start from scratch if you have to. In the long run, you only make more work for yourself by trying to salvage material, because an agent or an editor will either make you do the work or turn down the book outright. And remember, as I warned you in chapter two, the first draft of a novel will usually require an overhaul rather than a polish.

Troubleshooting

I suggest going through the same process for plot as you did for character—as you will for point of view, style and language. Put the first draft aside for a week. Then take it out and read it straight through. Make notes as you go but don't stop to rewrite. You want to read it as your readers will.

This is also a time when it can be extremely helpful to read your novel aloud to an audience. You may be in a writing group in which you do that already. But you may not be in a group (although, if you're not, you should be) or you may be in a group in which participants take home each other's manuscripts to read.

Actually, I prefer groups in which participants read each other's work at home. Overall, the criticism will be deeper, because every-one has more time to ponder what's working or not working about a manuscript, and really to think about their suggestions. They'll also be able to do a lot more line editing.

But you as author get something out of reading aloud that you can't get from people who read your work when you're not present. *You can see where you're losing your audience.* There's nothing like watching a young, gum-chewing woman shove her chair back and sigh to force you to confront the fact that the scene of Paul sipping pinot noir in a café and meditating on the nature of happiness is slow, or that the dialogue between Max and Kristi in which they discuss their failed relationship is too clunky.

So if you're not in a group that provides you a forum in which to read your work aloud, then find a friend or other victim to sit and listen. In this case you are not necessarily looking for another writer, who would be better equipped to give you advice, you are just looking for an audience so you can see in his face and body language where the story drags.

In both reading to an audience and reading to yourself, here are some particular areas and common problems in the area of plot that you should be looking for:

Beginning the Book Too Early

In *Get That Novel Started!* I dealt fairly extensively with the issue of how to begin one's novel, so I don't want to dwell on it too much here. But I will point out at this juncture that a common mistake that writers make is to begin their books too early. They feel they must produce endless background on the characters so that readers will know how those characters got to be how they are.

The section on rewriting really is the best time to address this issue, because often you really can't determine the best way to begin your novel until you've written a complete draft of it. It's far better to write thirty pages of absolute *drek* and then to write another thirty, and another, and another. Each thirty pages will be better than the thirty pages before and by the time you have three hun-dred or more you will feel little distress at cutting the first thirty, or at least that ten-page flashback out of chapter two.

It is axiomatic that the reader is always more interested in what's *going* to happen than in what happened before. Ask yourself, where does the story really start?—and then begin there.

Forwarding the Plot in Dialogue

Readers love dialogue; it brings them immediately into a scene. Good dialogue also will often forward the story in subtle ways.

You need to be wary, however, of dialogue that seems unreal because it too obviously delivers needed information. Although in real life people often offer long explanations or instructions, in a novel it can sound phony. What's even more problematic is a conversation in which two people tell each other things just because the author wants the reader to know them.

> "Well, I was born in Minnesota. Not a bad place to grow up, but cold."
>
> "How many siblings do you have?"
>
> "I had two younger brothers. Earl is a doctor in San Antonio and Bob is an accountant in Phoenix."
>
> "What about your your mom and dad? Are they still living?"
>
> "Yes. They're seventy and seventy-five, respectively."

This might work if someone is being interviewed for a job or newspaper article. But otherwise, you should keep in mind that most people, when talking, usually don't entirely stick to the subject. At the same time, their speech is full of hidden meanings and agendas. Even in a straightforward interview, the two people involved are likely to be acting out a number of other dramas. How do they feel about each other and what they're talking about? Is someone trying to avoid a particular topic, or paint himself as somewhat grander than he is?

An exception to this might be in a hardcore mystery. There you would be justified in writing passages of dialogue between the detective and someone else involved in this case in which they simply review the information and discuss possible avenues of investigation. In a more complex mystery, however, there will still be the characters to consider and what else they want from each other, besides just solving the crime.

Any Scene Without Conflict

Once in a while a student will ask me, in a shocked voice, "Does every scene need to have conflict?"

Yes.

Every scene, every paragraph, every sentence. That doesn't mean that each scene is two or more people quarreling. What it does mean is that at every moment of a novel a character wants something he or she can't have because of an obstacle, internal or external. The character might not even know she wants it, but she does.

So as you read your first draft, look for any time when the conflict is not apparent. Your first clue will be a faint impatience or even boredom on your part. And hey, this is your book, so if *you're* feeling bored, pay attention to that.

Good Motives Aren't Necessary but Well-Motivated Characters Are

Fictional characters are complex and are capable of acting in many different ways in many different situations. Just like real people: Sometimes I pass by a panhandler on the street; sometimes I give him a dollar. Sometimes I grin indulgently when my husband leaves a dirty cheese knife on the drainboard; sometimes I chase him with it.

But if you know your characters well, you'll know when they're behaving believably and when not. And don't ever let them behave out of character for the sake of the plot.

Some years ago I saw a movie, *Foul Play*, in which Goldie Hawn is being pursued by a killer. At one point, although knowing the killer is nearby, co-star Chevy Chase leaves her alone. When he said to her, "Wait here," it was so clearly a device to allow her to be stalked again, that the audience groaned aloud. I'm not exaggerating when I say it undermined the entire film.

Review the Principles

Ask yourself, are characters taking action to resolve conflict and thus creating new conflicts, or intensifying the old, or both? Are the stakes increasing from beginning to end? What is the premise, and have you proved it as best you can, not only through the main plots, but the subplots? Can you prepare us any better, through foreshadowing, for events as they unfold? Have you taken advantage of all the dramatic opportunities presented by the novel, while keeping it as tight as possible?

Writing a novel is such an exhausting process that I think it is almost inevitable that even the most fastidious author will look at her manuscript at some point and think, "Well . . . it's probably good *enough*." Good enough is rarely good enough in the highly competitive publishing industry. Get out the shovel and start digging again.

For *Get That Novel Started!* I formulated Levin's Rule of Rewriting, which was that you have to do one more draft than you think you can stand. Turns out I was wrong: You usually have to do *two* more drafts than you think you can stand. So you can't say I didn't warn you.

Additional Plot Exercises

1. Outline a sequel to a favorite book.

2. Do some brainstorming exercises with a partner. One of you invents a character and a situation: For example, "A sixty-year-old Stanford professor, happily married for years, falls madly in love with a graduate student." Then the other person invents what happens next. "He gives up his career and the two of them run away to Mexico." Then switch roles: The other person invents a character and situation which the first partner builds on.

You can continue the exercise. After the second partner describes how the professor and his former student run off to Mexico, the first partner can pick up the story and invent what happens there. See how many adventures you can come up with. It's OK to be silly; you're learning to spin tales.

3. Write down a memorable incident from your childhood. The night your mother told you your parents were getting a divorce; the time you were unfairly suspended from school; your grandfather's funeral. Now look at it in terms of plot. What are the conflicts? (Your parents want to get a divorce, you don't want them to.) Is anyone taking action to get what he wants? (You threaten to set fire to the house if they don't stay together.)

The actual facts of the incident will probably have little or no plot. But take those facts and shape them into one. The result need have no bearing on what really happened.

4. Look back at something you wrote a long time ago (or fairly recently, if you haven't been writing for a long time). Analyze it dispassionately, using the principles we've discussed. Is there conflict in every scene? Are the characters taking action? Is there a premise proved at the end? Think about how you might restructure the plot now.

CHAPTER FOUR

Where You Stand Depends on Where You Sit

Point of View

THE BASICS

Point of view is a less obvious, and less glamorous, element of a novel than character or plot. No one ever recommends a book to you exclaiming, "Man, the point of view will blow you away!" Nor can I recall ever seeing a jacket blurb that praised the author, "We always know whose head we're in."

It's too bad. Point of view is the overworked, underpaid servant of novel-writing. It slaves in the kitchen making the host and hostess—character and plot—look good out in the dining room.

You *can* write a novel without knowing much about point of view, and unfortunately, some authors do. But a sloppy use of point of view will disrupt the flow of your writing, lead you into repetition, and cause you to tell rather than to show.

Skillful use of point of view, on the other hand, can increase reader identification with characters, help you prove your premise, and intensify the experience of reading the novel. Meanwhile, it can impose a discipline that pushes you to a higher level of skill in characterization, plotting, even the use of language. In short, it shows that you know what you're doing, and even if the reader isn't consciously aware of how your skill is manifesting itself, he'll appreciate the results.

Your choice of point of view will greatly affect the mobility you give yourself as author. (By mobility in this context I mean the author's ability to convey information.) The point of view also heavily influences the opinions that the reader will form about the story: who should live, who should die, who should be boiled in oil—and who deserves to triumph.

Point of View Defined

At any one moment in a novel, there is a point of view. It is the position of the author or character telling the story at that moment.

If you write, "The sun was rising," someone is letting us know that the sun was rising. The point of view is that someone—the consciousness through which the action of the novel is filtered. Or, you could think of point of view as a camera, only it's a camera that can hear, taste, smell, touch and/or interpret as well as see.

The point of view may change many times or it may stay the same throughout.

Here are the basic types of point of view with a brief description, including some advantages and disadvantages of each (a simplified form of these definitions appears in *Get That Novel Started*):

First Person

In the first-person point of view the camera is in the head of a character in the novel. Reading a first-person novel is like hearing someone tell you a story: The character who is the first-person narrator refers to himself/herself as "I" and (often) to the reader as "you."

The Range of First Person

A sample of first-person point of view:

> You don't know about me, without you have read a book by the name of *The Adventures of Tom Sawyer*, but that ain't no matter. . . .
>
> Now the way that book winds up, is this: Tom and me found the money that the robbers hid in the cave, and it made us rich. . . . The Widow Douglas, she took me for her son, and allowed she would sivilize me; but it was rough living in the house all the time, considering how dismal regular and decent the widow was in all her ways; and so when I couldn't stand it no longer, I lit out.
>
> —Mark Twain, *The Adventures of Huckleberry Finn*

This passage illustrates perhaps the chief advantage of the first-person point of view: The character can address the reader directly, drawing him into the story. In first person, it's natural to cajole, joke, apologize, explain, persuade.

Thus the first person often adopts a conversational tone, as if the narrator is sitting with his friends around a campfire or in a living room, and kicking back to spin a tale. But this isn't always the case. A first-person narrator can also be formal, remote, academic. Kazuo Ishiguro's *The Remains of the Day* has such a first-person narrator. It begins:

> It seems increasingly likely that I really will undertake the expedition that has been preoccupying my imagination now for some days. An expedition, I should say, which I will undertake alone, in the comfort of Mr. Farraday's Ford; an expedition which, as I foresee it, will take me through much of the finest countryside of England to the West Country, and may keep me away from Darlington Hall for as much as five or six days.

The First-Person Narrator and "You"

The first-person narrator often addresses the reader directly as "you." As we've seen, *The Adventures of Huckleberry Finn* opens, "You don't know about me, without you have read a book by the name of *The Adventures of Tom Sawyer....*" Sometimes, especially when the tone is more formal, the first-person narrator addresses the reader directly without ever saying "you"—the *you* is implied. The narrator of *The Remains of the Day*, Stevens, never explicitly identifies the reader as his audience. Still, throughout the book, his tone is one of someone explaining himself: "I feel I should perhaps return a moment to the question of his lordship's attitude towards Jewish persons, since this whole issue of anti-Semitism, I realize, has become a rather sensitive one these days." Although the reader is not directly addressed, this is clearly a man defending himself to an audience, which in this case is the reader of the book.

Sometimes the "you" of the first person, that is, the person being addressed, is not the reader at all but another character in the novel. This would be the case in an epistolary novel, for example, in which the first person is the letter-writer and the person addressed is the recipient of the letter. It's true in a number of other novels as well, such as Gloria Naylor's *Mama Day*, in which two young people narrate portions of the novel, addressing each other. It's also the case in a book by Maureen Freely, *My Year With the Stork Club*: Here the narrator is an ex-husband who tells his side of the story of his infidelities, addressing his wife. "Sometimes ... I think I hear a child crying behind a closed door—or you in the bedroom, laughing on the phone."

The Narrator as Main Character ... Or Not

The first-person narrator of a novel is most often the main character of that novel. This is the case in all the examples of first-person novels quoted so far. It's natural to tell one's own story, after all; not to mention that no one knows more about one's own story than oneself.

But first-person narrators are also most often main characters because, since the action of a first-person novel is being filtered through the consciousness of one character in the book itself, the first person has the limitation that the narrator can only tell the reader information that the narrator herself knows. This makes it much more difficult for a first-person narrator to tell someone else's story. I can tell you an awful lot about my sister, after all, but still nowhere near what she can tell you herself.

However, there are reasons why you might choose someone other than the main character of your novel as its first-person narrator. Perhaps you want to portray someone through someone else's eyes; perhaps that person's limited knowledge of the main character will be enough for the story you want to tell. Or perhaps your main character wouldn't make a good first-person narrator, but you still want the immediacy of the first person.

The main character of *The Great Gatsby* is Jay Gatsby (at least, arguably), but the book is narrated by Nick Carraway. The mystery surrounding Gatsby is central to the novel itself. If Gatsby told the story, we'd obviously feel cheated that he was withholding information—that is, if he didn't tell us the truth about himself, including his shady past. Here, the suspense of the novel is heightened by the point of view.

Second Person

You are not the kind of guy who would be at a place like this at this time of the morning. But here you are, and you cannot say that the terrain is entirely unfamiliar, although the details are fuzzy. You are at a nightclub talking to a girl with a shaved head. The club is either Heartbreak or the Lizard Lounge. All might come clear if you could just slip into the bathroom and do a little more Bolivian Marching Powder.

—Jay McInerney, *Bright Lights, Big City*

This is the second person. It's almost the same as the first person: The camera is in the head of a character in the novel who tells the story. The difference is that instead of addressing the reader or another character in the novel, the narrator addresses himself. It's sort of like the way you might chastise or congratulate yourself as you walk down the street. "Now why did you wear these spike heels today? Your feet are going to snap off at the ankles. Although you do look sexy in them, I'll grant you that."

I said in the section on first-person point of view that the first-person narrator usually addresses the reader as "you." If he doesn't do so directly, then the "you" is implied. And when the "you," isn't the reader, it's another character in the novel.

But in the second person, the "you" of the first person *is* the first person. The loop closes in on itself, shutting us out. The character isn't telling his story to someone else, he's merely ruminating on how it affects him.

You can see then how the second person is a narcissistic point of view. It was perfect for the 1980s. *Bright Lights, Big City*, first published in 1984, popularized it, and many young writers of short fiction as well as novels followed suit. They were writing about self-absorbed people; it was natural that they address themselves.

Bright Lights, Big City is a fine book (as are many other works written in second person) but I don't think the second person has a bright future. Because it does shut the reader out, the second person does not engage us the same way that the true first person does. It's too much like listening to a teenager tell a story. "So, like, you know how it is at the mall, uh . . . " We are more like voyeurs than listeners, eavesdropping on someone's—*shudder*—interior monologue as he lives his life. But while the second person isn't as engaging, it suffers from the same lack of mobility as the first-person point of view.

Don't get confused by the "you." Occasionally (more often in a short story), the "you" will be the main character, but the narrator will be "I." For example, I recall hearing a short story in which a young woman imagines her lover creeping over to her house in the pre-dawn hours, staring at her window and then returning home. The story mostly described the young man, who was "you," but the "I" of the story was the young woman, and the story was written in the first person, not the second.

The point of view is always the consciousness filtering the action.

Third Person

Third person has several permutations. It can be single or multiple, and both the single and multiple can be either limited or omniscient.

Let's discuss the basic concept first. In third person the camera may be in the head of a character, but that character is described as "he," "she" or by his or her proper name.

Let's look at this excerpt from Joan Didion's *Play It as It Lays*. It's the beginning of chapter thirty-five. Maria Wyeth, the main character of the novel, is separated from her husband, depressed over a recent abortion and now living in a furnished apartment.

> "I don't know if you noticed, I'm mentally ill," the woman said. The woman was sitting next to Maria at the snack counter at Ralph's Market. "I'm *talking* to you."
>
> Maria turned around. "I'm sorry."
>
> "I've been mentally ill for seven years. You don't know what a struggle it is to get through a day like this."
>
> "This is a bad day for you," Maria said in a neutral voice.
>
> "What's so different about this day."
>
> Maria looked covertly at the pay phones but there was still a line. The telephone in the apartment was out of order and she had to report it. The line at the pay phone at Ralph's Market suddenly suggested to Maria a disorganization so general that the norm was to have either a disconnected telephone or some clandestine business to conduct, an extramarital error.

The camera is Maria's head. It reports what she sees, hears, tastes, touches, smells and thinks. ("Maria looked covertly at the pay phones. . . .") In the third person, no "you" is addressed (with one possible exception that we'll discuss.)

The most striking advantage of the third person over first is that the former has more mobility. As we'll see, in third-person multiple and third-person omniscient you as author have the opportunity to go beyond what one character knows.

In the third-person single, limited point of view you are bound by what one character knows in the same way that you are in first person. However, third-person single, limited is not like writing in the first person with the "I"s changed to "he"s. The third person creates more distance between the readers and the characters they are reading about. No one is saying, "Come, sit, I have a story to tell you."

More distance isn't necessarily bad, though. Sometimes we want it. Sometimes we need it. Maria Wyeth, in fact, is an example of a character from whom we need it. On a good day, Maria is extremely depressed and anxious. Didion's portrayal of her mental state is chillingly accurate. If we were drawn any more deeply into it than we are in third person, we might feel overwhelmed.

That doesn't mean that we are not expected to feel about the characters and the story; quite the contrary. But third person can make an otherwise too-uncomfortable reading experience tolerable.

Even when mobility is not an issue, third person can be preferable to first person when the hero or heroine of the novel is not someone from whom we want to hear the story.

Third-person limited, single can also have another advantage over first person. In the single third-person limited (which the excerpt from *Play It as It Lays* is), the author cannot directly tell us what the character doesn't know, just as in first person. But the author can go beyond what the same character could express for herself in first person. Maria is fairly inarticulate. If you string together her dialogue it looks like it came from a poorly punctuated Easy Reader. "Where." "The pain." "I read that." "Just a doctor. On Wilshire."

Granted that dialogue is not the same as first-person narration, we have even more evidence for the point in Didion's novel. *Play It as It Lays* has three prologues, written in the first person by Maria and two other important characters respectively. Maria's prologue reveals a mind disturbed and disjointed. She's desperately trying to stay in control. She's *not* lively, intelligent, funny, insightful or informative. Therefore, in third person, the author can be inside a character's head but not be as confined by that character's own limitations.

Third-Person Single vs. Third-Person Multiple

In the excerpt from *Play It as It Lays*, you can see that the camera is firmly planted in the head of a woman named Maria. In the sample quoted, and indeed in the rest of the book, we are always in Maria's head (with the exception of the two prologues mentioned that take the point of view of other important characters in the novel). When the camera remains in the head of one character throughout, the point of view is third-person single.

Many novels are written with a single third-person point of view. But many novels switch third-person points of view, making the point of view third-person multiple. In order to illustrate simply how it works, let's take the same passage from *Play It as It Lays* and imagine switching mid-scene from Maria's point of view to the point of view of the self-proclaimed mentally ill woman. I've bold-faced my changes.

"I don't know if you noticed, I'm mentally ill," the

woman said. The woman was sitting next to Maria at the snack counter at Ralph's Market. "I'm *talking* to you."

Maria turned around. "I'm sorry."

"I've been mentally ill for seven years. You don't know what a struggle it is to get through a day like this."

"This is a bad day for you," Maria said in a neutral voice.

"What's so different about this day."

The woman regarded Maria with suspicion. At first she had thought that Maria, who was thin and stylish, if a bit haggard, would be sympathetic, but now instead Maria was just talking like those two-bit shrinks down at the clinic.

She followed Maria's gaze to the pay phones. *She wants to make a call.* The woman was angry at Maria for thinking of her call instead of listening to her.

This is the third-person multiple point of view: At different points of the novel the camera reports the impressions of different characters.

The third-person single point of view definitely gives you more mobility than the first person, especially if you are writing in third-person omniscient, instead of limited. But you will still pretty much only be able to go where your one point of view character goes. Sometimes that won't be enough.

There's absolutely nothing wrong with writing a novel in which you take more than one character's point of view, although a few hard-core academic types will tell you otherwise. The number of points of view you decide to take depends on the book that you're writing.

In the last chapter we talked about a book called *Labor Pains*, in which five women go through pregnancy and childbirth. In order to render the experiences of each of the women, the author, Kate Klimo, pretty much had to take each woman's point of view. If Kate Klimo had wanted to write a book about one woman going through pregnancy and childbirth, she would have written a different book. Perhaps she would have delved more deeply into the experiences of that one woman. But apparently that wasn't the book she wanted to write. Apparently she wanted to write about five women in order to capture the spectrum of the modern pregnancy-and-childbirth experience, and the book is decent pop fiction.

Multiple points of view are not confined to pop fiction, though. Imagine *War and Peace* from the point of view of Natasha only. It

would still be the moving story of a young girl growing to woman-
hood, learning about life and love, but it would no longer be the
epic story of a nation in a time of crisis.

Only Take the Points of View You Need

So, yes, you can take all the points of view you need. The key
word here is "need."

Far too many beginning writers think that they can and should
pop in out of their characters' heads the way my husband jumps
from channel to channel when he watches TV with the remote
control. How else, these authors wonder, will the reader know what
the characters are feeling?

Lots of ways.

You're writing about a young woman going to her first dance.
You describe her getting dressed, arguing with her mother over her
decolletage, spritzing on perfume.

Now she arrives at the ball. So you think, I want to show the
reader that all the young men at the ball are attracted, and all the
young women are envious (granted, the men can be envious and
the women attracted, if you want to do it that way). So you decide
to take the point of view of several of the other guests, to narrate
their reactions as the young woman makes her entrance. *Wow*, someone thinks. *Cindy looks great!* And another: *I wish I had the figure to
wear that dress. . . .*

But suppose you stayed with Cindy's point of view. You write
about how her heart beats as she enters. Then you write about how
she observes conversations stopping as people turn to look at her.
Another young woman's hand goes to her own throat. A young man
bringing champagne to his date drops the glass.

Thus staying in Cindy's point of view forces you to observe for
yourself more subtle details—gestures, expressions, the way people
mask resentment by giving compliments. Staying in Cindy's point
of view forces you *to show rather than to tell.* So, often by staying in
a character's head rather than indiscriminately changing points of
view, you can actually push your writing to a higher level of skill.

Often, too, beginning novelists think that the best way to motivate a character is by taking that character's point of view. It may
be the easiest way, but it's not always the best.

Let's say you're writing about men and women manning a space
station on Jupiter. The bad guy is plotting to take over the station
and send the commander into orbit. But you want us to understand
why, so you take the bad guy's point of view so he can reflect on

his unhappy childhood when the bullies on the playground were mean to him, at which time he vowed never to let anyone take advantage of him again.

But if you've committed yourself to staying in the point of view of the commander, you can find other ways to motivate your character. You might have to dispense with the flashback to the villain's childhood, but most flashbacks to pivotal traumatic episodes from childhood are extremely expendable anyway. Perhaps, instead, the commander observes how the villain pays court to one of the female officers, who rebuffs him in favor of the commander himself. Thus you create a subplot that's of interest in the present. Once again, you are showing rather than telling. (Flashbacks to childhood generally equal telling.)

Besides eliminating opportunities to show, unnecessary point of view shifts disrupt our reading experience. When you write, you seek to simulate, to the extent possible, a real experience for the reader. This sense that events are unfolding as they would in real life is what John Gardner called "the fictional dream," a term that's become quite popular. One of the requirements of a successful fictional dream is that the narrative be "vivid and continuous," as Gardner himself put it. But when you switch points of view you create *dis*continuity. It's a speedbump in the reader's road. A point of view switch reminds us, however briefly, that we are reading a book.

By contrast, when you stay in one character's head for a length of time, the reader is more likely to identify with that character, or at least to believe that he exists.

Another pitfall of unnecessary switches is redundancy. To illustrate crudely, let's go back to the example of beautiful Cindy making her entrance at the dance. Likely as not, as she smooths her gown, she thinks, *I look pretty*. If the author takes the point of view of someone watching her enter, what is that character going to think? Maybe not, *she looks pretty*. Maybe, *she looks beautiful*. But you see the problem—we're getting information we already know.

That doesn't mean it's always better to stay in one character's head. I hope I made that clear. Maybe your novel has a subplot about another character at the same dance as Cindy's, and after her entrance you break the scene and pick up with that other character, in a different room, putting the make on a lady by the punch bowl.

Necessary point of view shifts can add layers of meaning. A classic example is the Japanese tale *Roshomon*, in which three people tell the same story of a couple's encounter with a thief in the woods.

Each version of the story is dramatically different, casting the narrator in the best possible light. In *Roshomon*, the three different points of view become the point of the story itself, which dramatizes how we all rationalize our own behavior.

But because of the risk of telling rather than showing, the disruption of the fictional dream, and the possibility of redundancy, you should never switch points of view out of laziness.

Avoid Switching Point of View Mid-Scene

When your novel requires multiple points of view, you will add unity and increase reader belief if you can stay in one point of view in each part (that is, a series of chapters) or at least each chapter. That isn't necessary, though, and often simply places too great a restriction on the story. However, you almost always want to stay in one point of view per scene.

Many successful pop fiction writers ignore this rule and flop around from head and to head according to their whim. There are more than a few literary novels that do the same. But I believe you have a lot to gain by following this rule, and I plan to argue the point thoroughly.

First of all, let's look at the concept of the scene itself. In one sense, a scene is an indivisible unit of a novel, because what makes a scene a scene is that it observes the unities of time, place and action. When the time or place changes, as a rule, the scene ends.

Staying in one point of view within the scene adds to the reality of the scene. When the scene breaks we're prepared to shift time and place—and point of view.

Glance back at the passage excerpted from *Play It as It Lays*, with which I took certain liberties. Without the boldface, you might not have realized that I had switched points of view until deep into the paragraph. When you switch points of view without a corresponding break in time and/or place, you invite such confusion.

Let's look at another example of how it doesn't work:

> Benjamin turned away from his mother. *She just doesn't understand*, he thought. He stared at the pictures of big-eyed children on the wall. Benjamin's mother, Jackie Sue, was also fond of clowns on velvet, but those were in the bedroom, with the Elvis night lamp.
>
> "I just don't see why you can't get another job in Greenville," she said. "Why you have to go all the way to New York."
>
> She disapproved of him. Benjamin stuck out his lower

lip. Jackie Sue didn't like to see him do that, it made him look like a five-year-old again—like a little boy who couldn't take care of himself.

We should always know whose consciousness is filtering the action. When the author (OK, so it was me) writes, *She just doesn't understand*, we know we're in Benjamin's head. And when we get to "Jackie Sue didn't like to see him do that, etc." we've switched to Jackie Sue. And just when was that switch made? The rest could have been in either character's head. The words, "She disapproved of him" could be Jackie Sue's true thoughts, or they could be Benjamin expressing his fear of what his mother thinks.

There's another reason not to switch mid-scene. Writing in the third-person point of view (especially third-person limited), you have the opportunity to capture the cadence and vocabulary of the character whose head you are in. Not as dramatically as you do in first person, but still.

Carson McCullers wrote *The Heart Is a Lonely Hunter* from multiple points of view. Here is a passage from the point of view of a one of the characters, a young girl called Mick:

> But maybe it would be true about the piano and turn out O.K. Maybe she would get a chance soon. Else what the hell good had it all been—the way she felt about music and the plans she had made in the inside room? It had to be some good if anything made sense. And it was too and it was too and it was too and it was too. It was some good.
>
> All right!
>
> Okay!
>
> Some good.

Although we read about Mick in the third person rather than the first, still we hear the rhythm of her thoughts expressed in her vocabulary. This excerpt ends the chapter. The next one begins:

> All was serene. As Biff dried his face and hands a breeze tinkled the glass pendants of the little Japanese pagoda on the table. He had just awakened from a nap and smoked his night cigar.

It's clear we're in a different character's head. In a multiple point of view novel, it's a good idea to create at least subtle differences in the thoughts and vocabulary of the characters, both to help orient the reader as you switch around, and for the sake of deeper characterization. But the separate voices that you use for different characters won't work unless you stay with one character until there's a break of time and/or place; in other words, until the end of the scene. If you try to do it within a scene, the writing will only seem muddled.

Third-Person Omniscient vs. Third-Person Limited

When you write in third person you have the option not just of single or multiple points of view, but of the omniscient or limited point of view. (Technically, the first person is always limited, unless your first-person narrator is a supernatural being of some sort.) I've referred to these two points of view already but now let's look at the choice in more detail.

Limited Point of View

In the limited point of view the camera is in a character's head only. That is, you can tell us just what that character knows, just as with the first-person point of view. Even so, the third-person limited is more mobile than first person, not only because the narration can go beyond the character's ability to express herself, but because it's more natural to interject knowledge that might be far from the character's thoughts at the moment. However, what the author does tells us at such a juncture does have to be something that the character knows.

Here's a sample of the limited point of view:

> Gloria walked down Main Street, noticing all the new shops that had opened that past year. For more than a decade Main Street—indeed, all of downtown Fairview—had been in decline. But since George Holman had opened the Girlz Club out by the river, soldiers had been pouring into town from the Army base and business was booming.

Presumably Gloria is an aware citizen of Fairview and knows the important goings-on; she may even have access to special knowledge that will equip her particularly well to be your point of view character. But let's look at it this way:

> Mama had told Gloria to put on her best Maryjanes, the ones that hurt Gloria's feet, because they were going to a place called Down-Town. When they got there, Gloria couldn't stop looking at all the dolls in the windows of the stores. And it wasn't even Christmas! The children who

lived in Down-Town were very lucky. Maybe they got new dolls every Sunday!

Now we are obviously in the head of a young child who would be unlikely to know the history of the town. As long as the point of view is limited, the author can't tell us more than what this child would know. If the author wishes to give us that information it will have to be through the point of view of another character, or the point of view will have to be omniscient.

Omniscient Point of View

In the omniscient point of view the camera is often in a character's head, but it can also pull back, to look at the bigger picture and give us information that the character doesn't know.

> It was a cold, clear day in Fairview. A woman in a heavy gray overcoat that had already been through many winters led a little girl down Main Street. The child excitedly looked in all the shop windows, while the woman trudged along, wondering whether she was going to have the rent money at the end of the week. Neither mother nor child noticed the pair of eyes watching them from the other side of the street.

Once again, you might assume at first that you have everything to gain and nothing to lose by writing in the omniscient rather than the limited point of view. If you consider just your ability to convey information to the reader, that's true.

But there are other factors to consider. In the passage about little Gloria, the limited point of view captures a little of the innocence of childhood. Downtown is a new, potentially exciting place. Dolls are infused with an importance they've lost for most adults. In other words, the limited point of view (like first person) can be more intimate, touching and real. As with first person, it is easier in some ways for the author to narrate from the point of view of a sophisticated, articulate and intelligent character, but sometimes a naive character is just the fresh perspective the author wants. By contrast, the omniscient point of view, while more informative in the strictest sense of the word, is also more neutral and more distancing than third-person limited—and thus engages us less.

It is in omniscient point of view that an author is most likely to "get away with" switching points of view mid-scene. In fact, that's just what happens in the passage above. But you can see how jerky it is, like watching a movie filmed with a hand-held camera. Even in omniscient point of view, it's a good idea to stay in one character's head for a length of time, for the duration of the scene when possible. While staying in that one character's head, you as omniscient author can still pull back to give us information that the character doesn't know:

> Jane put on her two-inch false eyelashes. She had no idea how ridiculous she looked.

Jane doesn't know how ridiculous she looks, so this is omniscient point of view. If you had chosen the limited point of view it might read:

> Jane put on her two-inch false eyelashes. *Mom says I look ridiculous but she's just jealous.*

As readers, we might infer that, jealous or not, Mom has a point.

Novels of previous centuries were more commonly written in the omniscient point of view than they are today. The modern novel has a psychological bent, just like modern society, and is given to explorations of individual minds. That doesn't mean that you can't explore psychology in the omniscient point of view: It was just as omniscient author that Tolstoy was able to bring such insight to his characters, telling us much more about them than they themselves knew. Nor does it mean that you can't document social problems in the limited point of view—look at *One Flew Over the Cuckoo's Nest* (written in first person, which is a limited point of view). But at some point our lens seems to have shifted from the god-position to the ground.

Note that although you can write as an omniscient author whether your novel has single or multiple points of view, the omniscient point of view combines more naturally with multiple points of view than it does with a single point of view.

Capturing the Character's Thoughts in Third-Person Omniscient

I've mentioned that an advantage of limited over omniscient point of view is that in the limited mode the author has a much broader opportunity to capture the voice of a character in the actual narration. Let me demonstrate how best to accomplish it in third-person omniscient. First, look at this passage:

> Mama had told Gloria to put on her best Maryjanes, because they were going to a place called Down-Town. When they got there, Gloria couldn't stop looking at all the dolls

in the windows of the stores. And it wasn't even Christmas!

Business in Fairview had been booming ever since George Holman had opened the Girlz Club out by the river, and soldiers had started pouring into town from the Army base.

Gloria saw a woman with gray hair like Grandma's sitting on a bench. But this woman had her own shopping cart from the grocery store. Maybe Gloria and Mama could bring one home so that Grandma could have one, too.

Well, maybe. But the trouble with this sample is that the shifts from Gloria's little-girl voice to the omniscient narrator's are rapid, frequent and therefore and potentially confusing, just like any mid-scene third-person shifts.

I think this is a better way to capture a character's thoughts in third person omniscient:

Gloria wished that Mama hadn't told her to put on her best Maryjanes, because they hurt her feet. But Gloria was a compliant child and so hobbled along without complaint.

Business in Fairview had been booming ever since George Holman had opened the Girlz Club out by the river, and soldiers had started pouring into town from the Army base.

Gloria saw people sitting in wrought-iron chairs at frosted-glass topped tables, eating ice cream. *Maybe Mama will let me have some, too,* she thought. *Ice cream is the bestest thing in the world.*

It is more difficult to give us Gloria's perceptions and vocabulary in third-person omniscient. But you can give us her italicized thoughts: *Ice cream is the bestest thing in the world.* Reporting some of the thoughts of the characters is a good way to soften the remoteness of the omniscient point of view, and to make the characters more vivid.

The Personal vs. the Impersonal Omniscient Point of View

When you write in omniscient point of view you have still another choice to make: whether to write as a *personal* or *impersonal* omniscient author.

The impersonal omniscient author establishes his ability to know everything at once but never his existence as a separate creature. He describes the action as a disembodied voice, all-knowing but uninvolved, kind of like a psychoanalyst. Any editorializing that he does do—and there often is some editorializing—is presented as fact.

> Only the expression of the will of the Deity, not dependent on time, can relate to a whole series of events occurring over a period of years or centuries; and only the Deity, prompted by no temporal agency, can by His sole will determine the direction of mankind's movement; man, however, is subject to time and himself participates in the event.
> —Leo Tolstoy, *War and Peace*

This is an omniscient narrator editorializing, but not identifying himself; that is, he doesn't refer to himself as "I."

The personal omniscient author, on the other hand, establishes herself as the consciousness telling the story. She refers to herself as "I" and the reader as "you," like a first-person narrator. (This is the exception, mentioned earlier, to the observation that there is no "you" in third person.) But the difference between a personal omniscient narrator and a first-person narrator is first, that the former is not a character in the story, while the latter is; and second, that the former is all-knowing while the latter is a human being limited by what humans know.

In novels of the eighteenth and nineteenth centuries, the personal omniscient author was common. He or she spoke to us directly, acknowledging his or her role as the author, as William Thackeray does in *Vanity Fair*: "It seems to me, for my part, that Mr. Rawdon's marriage was one of the honestest actions which we shall have to record in any portion of that gentleman's biography. . . ."

Modernly, the personal omniscient author is quite rare, so rare that to write in such a point of view attracts a good deal of attention to itself. But that doesn't make it bad. In *The Unbearable Lightness of Being*, author Milan Kundera writes as a personal omniscient author:

> I have been thinking about Tomas for many years. But only in the light of these reflections did I see him clearly. I saw him standing at the window of his flat and looking across the courtyard at the opposite walls, not knowing what to do.

Tomas is the main character of Kundera's book. Elsewhere this personal omniscient author (who is not necessarily Kundera himself, though we'll naturally link the two) writes of another character: "I sometimes have the feeling that her entire life was merely a continuation of her mother's, much as the course of a ball on a billiard table is merely the continuation of the player's arm movement."

Kundera is stepping out of the action to remind us that this is a novel. (That makes his book metafiction, by the way—a term that refers to fiction that acknowledges itself as fiction, rather than posing as truth.). He's inviting us to share in his creative process. To what end? In this case, I think that the personal omniscient author is a kind of political statement. Kundera is writing about a time and place in which artists are subjected to serious restrictions. He's letting us experience how fragile, and how precious, artistic creation is.

You may decide to write as a personal omniscient author for other reasons. Fay Weldon uses it in her novel, *The Heart and Lives of Men*, which begins, "Reader, I am going to tell you the story of Clifford, Helen and little Nell."

This opening has all the charm of the best first-person narration, telling us to pull up our chairs and get comfortable, for an interesting tale is at hand. Weldon's personal author appears occasionally, usually at the beginning of the chapter, and never gets much more personal than that. The point of view also adds to the exceedingly wry tone that is a trademark of Weldon's novels.

For the drawback of this point of view, let me quote Leon Surmelion, in *Techniques of Fiction Writing: Measure and Madness*:

> When the writer addresses the reader, he underscores his presence. The event did not happen by itself, as events happen in life. Somebody stage-managed the affair, it is a puppet show. To make imitation seem true: that is the challenge in this craft. . . .
>
> The writer's presence will not invariably destroy the illusion of reality, but some damage is always done.

Non-experimental novels of the twentieth century generally attempt to be more natural, that is, to simulate reality. Either in first or third person, we are asked to believe that what we are reading is real. We don't expect to be addressed directly; it may jar us when we are.

But who knows that the personal omniscient author won't come back into fashion? If it does, it will be different from the personal omniscient authors of old, just as any fashion, when revived, has slightly different lines.

The External Point of View

Imagine the camera sitting on a tripod, indifferently recording the action.

> One evening of late summer, before the nineteenth cen-
> tury had reached one third of its span, a young man and
> woman, the latter carrying a child, were approaching the
> large village of Weydon-Priors, in Upper Wessex, on
> foot. . . .
> [The couple] walked side by side in such a way as to
> suggest afar off the low, easy, confidential chat of people
> full of reciprocity; but on closer view it could be discerned
> that the man was reading, or pretending to read, a ballad
> sheet which he kept before his eyes with some difficulty by
> the hand that was passed through the basket. Whether this
> apparent cause were the real cause, or whether it were an
> assumed one to escape an intercourse that would have been
> irksome to him, nobody but himself could have said pre-
> cisely; but his taciturnity was unbroken, and the woman
> enjoyed no society whatever from his presence.
>
> —Thomas Hardy, *The Mayor of Casterbridge*

This is the external point of view. The facts alone are recorded by a neutral observer who can see and hear, and document the other sensory experiences of touch, smell and taste to the extent that a neutral observer would.

In the excerpt from *The Mayor of Casterbridge*, admittedly, the report isn't exactly neutral. When Hardy writes, "The woman en-joyed no society whatever from his presence," we can infer his disapproval of the man. What makes this point of view external is that the narrator can't see into anyone's head. Ultimately, he's merely reporting the fact that the man and woman aren't speaking to one another. He has no advantage over what the reader would have if the reader were there, and he invites the reader to draw any conclusions that she wishes—even if he might nudge our conclu-sions in one direction or the other.

Choosing a Point of View

Sometimes choosing a point of view is easy—so easy that you don't know that you're doing it. You walk around wondering if you dare to begin a novel, thinking of the work involved, the self-exposure, the time away from your garden. Then the first sentence comes to you, "Whether I shall turn out to be the hero of my own life, or whether that station will be held by anyone else, these pages must show." Or, "It is a truth universally acknowledged that a single man in possession of a good fortune must be in want of a wife." Relieved, gratified and scared to death, you sit down to write, having chosen your point of view in the process.

Probably a slight majority of first-time novelists feel more comfortable with first person. First person lends itself not only to storytelling, but to confession—and that first novel is often a story that the writer needs to unburden herself of. But plenty of first-timers work more naturally with third person. I did, starting out; but now find I drift more to the first. Can't say why.

I've occasionally heard that editors are prejudiced against the first-person point of view in first novels, because they suspect it leads the author into self-indulgence. That is a possible pitfall of the first-person, but the potential gains are there, too: a first-person novel can be honest and original. I believe strongly that point of view choices depend on the individual book and the individual writer. First isn't better than third, nor vice versa. Imagine *Huckleberry Finn* or *Catcher in the Rye* in the third person. ("Huck Finn was a mischievous boy who went around barefoot with a straw dangling from his mouth. . . .") Imagine *Anna Karenina* in the first. ("I couldn't help but notice that dashing cavalry officer at the train station. What a hunk! Don't get me wrong. I'm a happily married woman. Well, somewhat happily. . . .")

If your point of view presents itself naturally, then follow that impulse, bearing in mind that you might make a conscious decision to change it later, perhaps as a way of shaking yourself loose when you feel stuck, on the suggestion of a colleague, or just to see what happens.

When the point of view does not present itself easily to you, then weigh these factors:

• Whose story is it? That person or those persons will often be the point of view character or characters, and often you won't need any more points of view than his, hers or theirs.

If you're not sure whose story this is, then ask yourself, who is most affected by the events? More importantly, who causes the events of the novel? Who takes up the most page time? *And who changes as a result of the action of the novel?*

If your novel tells the story of more than one person, and those characters have relatively equal weight in the story, then you are probably looking at multiple points of view, usually third, but possibly first, or even mixing first and third, a technique we'll discuss further, later in this chapter.

Characters do not need to equal the main character in importance in order to deserve to be point of view characters. Sometimes the point of view of a secondary character is simply crucial to telling the story. The key words here are "simply crucial." Ask yourself, to what extent will I be straitened in my efforts to tell the story if I *don't* take this character's point of view?

For example, you're writing about the dedicated director of a private nursing home who's trying to improve the level of care in spite of a selfish management who only cares about keeping the bottom line high. You have a subplot concerning an elderly woman, recently arrived, who's trying to adjust to life in the home, while her family visits her less and less often.

You may decide to stick to the nursing home director's point of view. It will increase her stature if she's able to empathize with the elderly woman's plight to the extent that we can feel what she's feeling without being inside her head.

But suppose the subplot concerning the elderly woman also involves a conspiracy on the part of some of her heirs to get her to rewrite her will in their favor. Then maybe—maybe—you will need her point of view and even the point of view of other members of her family.

• If you have a single main character, but you're debating between first and third person, ask yourself, is this main character a person with whom I'd like to be marooned on a desert island? A main character may have plenty of stature, complexity and goals that she can act upon, and therefore qualify easily for the job of protagonist—and yet not be someone who can tell her story well or sympathetically. (We've discussed Maria Wyeth and Scarlett O'Hara as an examples of this.)

• Another consideration in point of view choice is the length and scope of the novel. The more pages a novel has, the longer the time period and the more places it covers, the more points of view you are likely to need.

• A historical novel may benefit from the omniscient point of view. Usually the social and political forces at work play a role in shaping the characters and the story, and the omniscient point of view allows the author more easily to give us the historical background we need.

• If you've always written in first person, or third-person multiple, or third-person limited—why not try a different point of view? You may discover new aspects of your writing ability.

These are considerations only. There are no easy calculations to make when it comes to choosing a point of view. But it *is* worth thinking about that choice, because the point of view influences so much in your novel—the voice, the characterizations, the story itself.

And don't overlook the opportunities to create subtle or dramatic effects, and layers of meaning, with some of the variations we'll discuss in the next section.

THE FINER POINTS

Multiple First-Person Narrators

In the majority of books written in first person there is only one first-person narrator throughout. But that's not a rule—a number of books take multiple first-person points of view.

An example of this technique is Amy Tan's *The Joy Luck Club*, in which seven different women narrate sixteen different chapters. Another example is William Faulkner's *As I Lay Dying*, in which a family journeys to bury their deceased matriarch, a powerful woman named Addy. Each chapter is told in the first-person point of view by one of Addy's children, her husband or one of a couple of neighbors; the middle chapter of the book is narrated by Addy herself.

The Joy Luck Club illustrates the major pitfall of multiple first-person narrators. The book is summarized briefly in chapter three, but here let me remind you that the story is narrated by a set of three mothers and a set of four daughters (one of the mothers is deceased at the time of the novel). It's easy for us as readers to distinguish between mothers and daughters, but not as easy to distinguish *among* the mothers and daughters; they tend to blur.

This difficulty in *The Joy Luck Club* arises in part from one of its strengths: The book is tightly focused on the mother-daughter relationship, and we tend to think of the characters in their roles as one of these.

That's one of the reasons *As I Lay Dying* better escapes the problem. Since the first-person narrators are Addy's children, her widower and the neighbors, their different relationships to her and to each other make them distinct. But even though each narrator speaks in the same regional dialect, and most have the tendency to repeat certain observations almost obsessively, Faulkner also endows the characters with subtly different ways of talking, which further delineates them.

However, the risk that first-person narrators will sound alike can be well worth taking in exchange for what the author may gain: the immediacy of first person combined with the mobility of multiple points of view. The power of *As I Lay Dying* is in the complex picture of a family and a subculture that emerges as different members reveal their impressions and secrets to the reader. Similarly, the cumulative tales of the mothers and daughters in *The Joy Luck Club* provide a more intricate and varied picture of the Chinese-American experience than just one point of view could.

Mixing First and Third Person

Another, more challenging, way to mix points of view is by combining first and third person.

What makes this combination more challenging is that the basic assumptions and conventions of first and third person are dramatically different. In first person, a character from the story is addressing you directly; in third person, usually an indifferent narrator documents the action, ignoring the reader. First and third are two different glosses on reality. However, my impression is that this device is becoming more common.

However, mixing the two *can* work, and when it works, it works beautifully. The very best example of mixing third and first person I ever read was in an unpublished novel. (There may be similar examples in published fiction with which I am unacquainted.) The hero of the novel is in the grip of a psychosis, and the story is told in third person. After the psychosis passes, he picks up the story in first person. He's able to be his true self.

In this case the point of view change dramatized the change in his mental state. The psychotic man was watching his own life as if it were a movie; when he recovers, he's able to participate in it once again.

Joan Didion also makes it work in *Play It as It Lays*. As noted earlier, that novel begins with three prologues, each a first-person narration by three different characters in the novel: Maria, her ex-husband and a friend (although the word "friend" is applied loosely throughout the novel, which depicts a friendless world). These prologues (all but Maria's are quite short) give us the flavor of each character's voice and lend some immediacy to what is the otherwise remote tone of the novel; at the same time the characters' slightly defensive explanations of what went wrong is consistent with its documentary style. A very brief, italicized epilogue returns to Maria's first-person point of view.

How to Get Around the Limits of the First Person

Whether your first-person narrator is the main character of your novel or a secondary one, at some point you will likely chafe against the constraints of that point of view. The fact that you can tell the reader only what that first-person narrator knows is a significant limitation. It makes storytelling more difficult, and it can stick you with a novel that seems claustrophobic. Fortunately, there are ways to work around this restriction.

Stories Within Stories

Let's look at *Wuthering Heights* to see how Emily Brontë does it. Narrator Ellen Dean, the faithful servant, is present at many of the key scenes in the novel. But in order to accomplish the scope of the narrative that she does, Brontë must include many passages in which other characters summarize events for Ellen so that Ellen can learn, and in turn tell us, what she hasn't witnessed but that we need to know.

For example, fairly early in the novel, young Heathcliff and Cathy can't be found one evening. Finally the house goes to bed; only Ellen waits up, worried. Eventually Heathcliff returns, without Cathy. He then gives Ellen a very detailed account of how he and Cathy stumbled upon the Linton estate, were set upon by the dogs and how Cathy was taken in by the Lintons, with the intention of keeping her there until the wound she received from one of the dogs can heal.

Heathcliff's story is actually a scene, though not as fully realized as many in the novel: It includes dialogue and many concrete details.

In real life, Heathcliff could probably not reconstruct the scene with such particulars, or tell it so smoothly. But he does, and we believe it, because that is a convention of novel writing. (A convention is a customary practice, and in the case of novels, it sometimes applies to a device that is not lifelike but that we've all agreed to overlook. Simply because it *is* commonly done, it becomes easier to overlook.)

This convention is an extension of the convention of the first-person narration itself: After all, Ellen Dean is telling Lockwood the story of Cathy, Heathcliff, et al. in the same or greater detail in which Heathcliff tells Ellen what happened that night. This question would arise in any first-person narration: Could Holden Caulfield have remembered his trip home from prep school in such detail? Could Huck Finn have reconstructed his and Jim's meeting with the Duke and the Dauphin word for word? Not likely.

As an aside, let's observe that sometimes a character shores up the likelihood of his phenomenal recollections with an occasional reference to the journal he kept at the time, or with a reminder of how important these events were to him, thus how memorable. In *The Great Gatsby*, Nick refers to having jotted down the names of the people who showed up at Gatsby's parties on a train schedule. That's a nice touch, but the truth is that much more of our lives are lost than would ever permit writing a novel based entirely on memory, even if we took a lot of notes.

Granted, though, that while the convention of the first-person narration remains, such speechifying as Heathcliff and other characters do in *Wuthering Heights* isn't as acceptable as it once was. If Brontë were writing today, rather than include long passages of actual speech, she might be more likely to use another technique of Fitzgerald's in *The Great Gatsby*: In one scene, Gatsby tells first person narrator Nick Carraway "a lot about the past"—which information Nick then summarizes for us. He gives us two paragraphs—but you can go on for much longer and in greater detail if you want, even to the point of dramatizing the story that the other person is telling, perhaps with occasional reminders to the readers of the process to which they owe the scene: "Lewis told me that he was perspiring from exertion."

You are remaining in first person, but expanding upon its limitations at the same time.

Letters and Diaries

A time-honored device for inserting a different point of view into a first-person novel is to let the first-person narrator receive a letter or find a diary that is then reprinted in the novel itself. If the letters and/or diaries are long and/or many, this in effect gives the novel another first-person narrator.

The device of letters and diaries is so time-honored, in fact, that if you use it you must be careful that it doesn't seem too convenient. And, since letters and diaries are far less common in modern life than they once were, you can expand the same device to include faxes, e-mail and very long messages on answering machines.

The Attributive Point of View

Another, albeit trickier, method is what I call the "attributive" point of view. This is where the first-person narrator imaginatively reconstructs a scene in which she was not present. That is, the narrator is *attributing* experience to someone else. Often the context indicates that we should believe the attribution and take it on authority. Other times the attributive point of view can add a dreamlike or speculative quality to the events described.

One example of the attributive point of view is in parts of F. Scott Fitzgerald's unfinished novel, *The Last Tycoon*. The book is narrated in first person by Cecilia Brady, a young woman who is the daughter of a Hollywood producer, but the main character is Monroe Stahr, also a producer, and a partner of Cecilia's father. Fitzgerald writes many scenes from Stahr's point of view in which Cecilia does not appear. For the most part these scenes are reconstructed by Cecilia based on reports from other people, but Cecilia also casually mentions at least once that she's supplementing with her imagination. In either case, Stahr's thoughts would be difficult for anyone to know, and yet they're included.

Once Fitzgerald establishes that Cecilia can reconstruct Stahr's experiences, he doesn't need to explain how she does it each time he takes Stahr's point of view. There are conventions of the novel in general, and then there are conventions of each individual novel. Your job is to set up your conventions early on and with authority and the reader will go along with them.

Another, rather different, example of the attributive point of view is Fay Weldon's novel, *Life Force*. This story is told by two women, Marion and Nora, who each speak in first person in alternating chapters, but in the second chapter, narrated by Nora, Nora tells us that *she* is the one writing Marion's chapters, imagining how Marion would tell her side of the story that involved Marion, Nora, their spouses, children and friends.

One could argue that *Life Force* is closer to being a book with two first-person narrators, but there's a additional purpose in having Marion's point of view filtered through Nora's. In *Life Force* Weldon is examining, in part, the way we try to control our lives through fiction. The book has, in effect, two endings: one more realistic but also sadder, in which marriages dissolve and people are left estranged and lonely; and another, which Nora imagines just as she imagines Marion's point of view, in which loose ends are tied up happily.

You can use the attributive point of view in much smaller ways than Fitzgerald or Weldon do. Suppose a man has recently separated from his wife. Alone in his studio apartment he thinks of her:

> She wanders about our house, picking up objects—old pictures, an ashtray from the Holiday Inn. None have the power to hurt her any more. She sits in the old chair and watches the fire. The flames leap up. Sparks fly.

This estranged husband doesn't know that this is what's going on at home. Depending on the character and the context, we readers might think that his depiction is accurate, but we also might think his account is influenced by his own fears and wishes.

The Careful Shift

In any novel with more than one point of view, it's important that the reader follow all your point of view shifts, and always know whose head you are in.

Sometimes your prose will immediately alert the reader. For example, a sentence beginning with "I" is a pretty good clue that you've shifted from third to first person.

Other times it won't be so obvious. Again, this is one of the reasons that it's important to stay in one point of view per scene. Once you've established that your novel is written in multiple points of view, the reader will be on the alert that when you change scenes you may also change points of view.

Even with the reader looking for a new point of view, you have to make it clear in whose head you've taken up residence. As soon as you make the shift, tell us something that the character is thinking or experiencing physically so that we can get grounded. That doesn't mean that every scene should begin with "Isaac thought" or "Beryl's jacket was itchy." But don't go on for pages and pages (or even paragraphs and paragraphs) describing the ocean or the woods without letting us know who is experiencing that ocean or that wood.

I've already mentioned that each third-person or first-person narrator will ideally have at least a slightly different way of thinking or speaking, a way that reflects his or her character and background. In the first sentence of the new point of view section, exploit the personal voice of the character to signal the point of view change.

For example, let's say you're writing a novel with two third-person point of view characters, one a father and one a teenage daughter. Either character might be likely to observe, "It was raining." But to alert the reader to the switch, you can reach for the more idiosyncratic way the characters would express themselves. In the daughter's point of view, write, "She was so damn sick of the rain," and in the father's, "What a harsh winter."

Juggling multiple first-person narrators can be among the most demanding for writer and reader. In some books the first-person narrators tend to sound alike, and since the first-person narrator is addressing the reader as "I," it may not be natural to squeeze in that narrator's proper name. ("I was back at the ranch, and I said to myself, 'Big Pete, it's time to feed them cows.' ")

One technique is to refer immediately to something in that first-person narrator's life that distinguishes this first-person narrator from the others in the novel. This is what I'm trying to do in my novel-in-progress, *Goodnight Light and the Red Balloon.* The novel has three first-person narrators, two sisters and their mother, so the characters have similar backgrounds. However, they have very different lives: The main character, Robin, has recently had a baby; her sister, Amy, is a single woman going rapidly from boyfriend to boyfriend, and their mother, Frances, is struggling with whether to stay with or to leave an unfaithful husband. So, Robin's sections often begin with a reference to the baby; one of Amy's sections begins with the despairing exclamation, "Guys!"; and Frances often announces her presence as point of view character with a reference to how things have changed since her children were little.

William Faulkner solves the problem in part in *As I Lay Dying* by labeling his chapters with the name of the narrator. Many novels similarly label chapters or parts with the name of the point of view character. This can be a good supplementary device, especially in a book such as his with so many narrators. But Faulkner doesn't use it as a substitute for keen character development, and you shouldn't, either.

Establishing the Omniscient Point of View

If you're writing as an omniscient author, you have to establish that perspective within the first few pages (if not sooner); otherwise when you step in to deliver information that the characters don't know, it will not only smell of convenience, it will jolt the reader who may have been making different assumptions about the world you've created.

An easy way to establish the omniscient point of view is to open a scene with a long shot, that is, to put the camera back where only an omniscient narrator is likely to be: "It was a sunny April morning, and a crowd had gathered around the County Courthouse."

Another way is by making commentary that goes beyond the level of insight of the characters, or just plain contradicts their thoughts. "Gene thought himself a better pitcher than he was, and he overlooked his tendency to miss fly balls."

Gene by definition can't tell us that he thinks himself a better pitcher than he is, because then he wouldn't think it. "He overlooked" also alerts us to the omniscient point of view: In limited point of view, you can't tell us what a character has overlooked. Of course, you may imply this information it in some fashion: "Gene figured that everyone missed a few fly balls now and then."

Here's a sample of how George Eliot describes her heroine Dorothea Brooke in *Middlemarch*: "She was . . . not in the least self-admiring; indeed, it was pretty to see how her imagination adorned her sister Celia with attractions altogether superior to her own. . . ." Dorothea can't know that she only imagines Celia more attractive than she.

Naturally, you must be careful, especially in a modern novel, not to let these types of observations become too ponderous. Eliot's many asides about her characters and their actions ("Destiny stands by sarcastic with our *dramatis personae* folded in her hand.") would not go down as easily today.

The Unreliable Narrator

This term often comes up in writing classes with a literary bent. An unreliable narrator is a first-person narrator whose judgment is so skewed or impaired that we as readers are meant to understand something different than what that narrator tells us.

An omniscient narrator—personal or impersonal—is by definition always entirely reliable. We may disagree with that narrator's opinions, but we have to believe that she means what she says, or the novel makes no sense.

In third-person limited our awareness that we are in the head of a fallible human injects a level of healthy scepticism into our reading. And once we get to first person, the transition is complete: We know that we are hearing only one side of the story. We know that Holden Caulfield can't bring the wisdom acquired in old age to his narrative, that David Copperfield (being male) will have an imperfect understanding of what women want, that the immigrant mothers of *The Joy Luck Club* see the United States differently from their American-born daughters.

So, in that sense, all first-person narrators are a little bit unreliable. But some are more so than others. Mark Twain establishes

Huck Finn's streak of unreliability on the very first page when Huck writes about the difficulties of being "sivilized," which include such hardships as sleeping in a house instead of a barrel. Since most of us would prefer the house to the barrel, we know right away that we're dealing with someone with different values from the average reader. Later Twain gets us to sympathize with the slave Jim's plight through the paradox of Huck's guilt about helping Jim escape:

> It was awful thoughts, and awful words, but they was said. And I let them stay said; and never thought no more about reforming. I shoved the whole thing out of my head; and said I would take up wickedness again, which was in my line, being brung up to it, and the other warn't. And for a starter, I would go to work and steal Jim out of slavery again; and if I could think up anything worse, I would do that, too; because as long as I was in, and in for good, I might as well go the whole hog.

Huck believes that he's doing wrong, because he's been taught that owning slaves is all right, and that abolitionists are evil fanatics. But it's quite clear that Mark Twain, the author, feels another way. This is one example of how an author can communicate something other than what the first-person narrator knows. *Huckleberry Finn* is full of scenes which the reader understands differently from Huck. (The vignette of a deceased adolescent girl whose pictures Huck admires is among the funniest.)

Unreliable narrators and tour de force novels go hand-in-hand. The challenge to the author is to keep the main character likable (since it's a first-person narrator, it's more important that he or she be likable) in spite or his or her naivete or self-delusions. Meanwhile, the author has to find a way to convey the true meaning behind the narrator's descriptions. In the hands of someone less skilled, Huck Finn would just be a bigoted bumpkin.

REWRITING NOTES

When to Rewrite From a Different Point of View

Rewriting an entire book from a different point of view, or adding or subtracting points of view, will seem a daunting task and you may try to avoid it—begging, pleading and arguing with yourself as you read that the book *really* doesn't need a different point of view.

Fortunately, it usually doesn't.

A book that isn't working is more likely to be not working because the plot is slow, the characters are inadequately revealed and/or the prose isn't polished enough. In fact, you should be wary of the trap of altering your point of view as a way of avoiding those even more daunting rewrites.

And be careful of editors who suggest point of view changes because they don't know what else to suggest. Point of view is the kind of subject that gets discussed at length in graduate school, and some editors will grab hold of it because no one taught them the mechanics of plot.

Since a different point of view is a different story, a change in point of view might create as many problems as it solves. When you go into a character's head whose point of view you haven't taken before, for example, that character tends to demand a subplot all his own; also, that character often needs to grow in a way that a non-point of view character doesn't.

And while switching from first to third person might solve a problem with self-indulgence, you might lose the engaging voice of your first-person narrator.

However, once in a while, point of view changes are what your novel needs. Here are some of the signs:

• Is the tone of your novel too remote? Since the point of view is the consciousness filtering the story, it is closely related to tone, which is the attitude of the author toward the material. We've seen that third person, and particularly third-person omniscient, are more distancing points of view than first person and third-person limited. A downshift to a more intimate point of view can address the problem of too much distance.

• Sometimes too-sensational material can benefit from more distance. If your novel of crimes of passion, sin, redemption and cannibalism threatens to overwhelm the reader, you can *up*shift to a more remote point of view—or you can choose a non-major character to tell the story. For example, a concerned aunt as narrator of the story of an abused child may be more palatable than that same story told from the point of view of the child.

This is in part what Ken Kesey accomplishes by choosing Chief as the narrator of *One Flew Over the Cuckoo's Nest*. Chief is seriously disturbed, but that same illness causes him to regard the frightening goings-on around him at some remove. He's invested in the battle between MacMurphy and Big Nurse, but less so than the principals, and therefore able to tell their story more objectively.

• Are the characters repeating themselves and your message? If the book feels too long, or padded, it's possible that you have a point of view character who can go: That point of view character might be the bearer of a subplot that isn't fully integrated into the whole.

In any book with multiple points of view, it never hurts to look at each point of view to make sure it contributes to the novel. So always ask yourself, is this point of view really necessary? And, is this point of view *switch* really necessary?

• More rarely, a book that feels thin can benefit from an additional point of view to shed more light on the action. But, generally speaking, I think it's better to go deeper than to go wider.

Once again, don't dither with the point of view in lieu of writing dramatic scenes, creating strong conflicts among the characters, selecting pithy details and writing sharp dialogue. But if you do decide to change the point of view (and please do, if that's what's needed!) then remember that it won't be a question of mechanically going through a manuscript and changing "I" to "she" or vice versa. Enter the new consciousness that's telling the story; regenerate the vocabulary, and the story itself.

Point of View Lapses

Although it doesn't very often happen that a writer has chosen the "wrong" point of view for her novel, what does often happen is that she slips out of it. Even a writer with a solid understanding of point of view can lose her footing once in a while.

Some years ago I took a photography class. The instructor asked us to do a series of photos on one subject, and one of my classmates shot rolls of film of some of the homeless people who made up a significant part of the population in San Francisco.

The night we hung our photos on the wall the instructor stopped at my classmate's display. "You shot these with a telephoto lens," she observed, pointing to a picture of a man sleeping in an empty refrigerator box.

"That's right," my classmate said, "I was afraid to get too close."

To which the instructor replied, "The fear shows in the picture."

Being new to photography I hadn't identified the odd perspective of the picture with the distortion that comes from using a telephoto lens. But I knew that something had bothered me about the picture—and now I knew what it was.

Point of view lapses will affect the reader the same way. He may not be conscious of the lapse, but he'll know something's wrong.

Even if you're so bold that you plan to ignore the no-mid-scene shift rule, then you still want to make your shifts on purpose. When you go back to re-read that first draft, look for places where you may have fallen out of point of view. Let's troubleshoot a few:

1. *Noelle was crying in the kitchen when she heard Charlene approach. Quickly, she reached for an onion and started chopping, to give herself an alibi for her tears.*

Charlene wasn't fooled for a moment by the onion. She silently put her arm around Noelle.

If the novel is being written from Noelle's point of view in that scene, then the sentence "Charlene wasn't fooled for a moment by the onion" is a point of view lapse, a shift to Charlene. Even if we're going to have Charlene's point of view later in the novel, this mid-scene, mid-moment shift is unnecessary. Just tell us that Charlene silently puts her arm about Noelle, and we'll see that Charlene wasn't fooled by the onion.

2. A novel is being written from the point of view of a little girl. The author describes, from that child's perspective, a fight between the parents that sends the father driving off furiously into the night:

Daddy was madder than Phoebe had ever seen. So mad that she wondered if he'd even come back this time.

An hour later, the children were all asleep.

"The children were all asleep" takes us out of Phoebe's point of view, because Phoebe wouldn't think of herself as "the children." What would work better would be something like, "An hour later, Mama made her and Tom go to bed."

3. A limited point of view novel describes a conversation between two friends, Joe and Mac, from Joe's point of view. The author writes, "A look of joy flitted across Joe's face." Since Joe can't see his own face, this is a point of view lapse. The author might convey the same information with, "He was joyful."

4. *Gertrude smiled at Paul, although she still felt nervous. "So we're friends again, aren't we, Paul?" she asked.*

Paul nodded, and offered his hand.

When George walked in a moment later, he was surprised to see Paul and Gertrude carrying on a lively conversation.

I give you this example to illustrate once again how easy it can be to render the same information without a point of view shift.

In the last sentence, all you have to do is write, "George *appeared* surprised to see Paul and Gertrude carrying on a lively conversation," to stay in Gertrude's head.

5. A friend of mine was writing a science fiction novel set a hundred years in the future. There were two third-person limited point of view characters, one an artificial human who had been manufactured by the government (which apparently will be in that business in the late twenty-first century), and the other a futuristic, hard-boiled private eye.

When the author wanted to step in to give the reader background as to the history of those future one hundred years, he made sure to put them in sections told from the viewpoint of the private eye, who, hardboiled or not, was an educated man who knew his history. When the author once slipped up and put this background in a scene told from the viewpoint of the artificial human, whose education and experience were minimal, that was a lapse. (I was very nice when I pointed it out.)

An alternative in a novel such as this would be to establish the presence of an omniscient author. The writer could do that early on with a sentence as simple as, "Blanche 608X didn't even know it was her birthday."

6. Sam and Brenda are talking at a party:

Brenda nodded. "I need another drink." She disappeared, heading towards the kitchen. There, she had to dive her hand into a ice-filled plastic garbage bin to get to the beer.

"She disappeared," indicates that we are in Sam's point of view, watching Brenda disappear, but then immediately we are in Brenda's head, as she sticks her hand into the big plastic garbage bin. (Even if this were written in the omniscient point of view, the jerk of the camera would throw us.)

Out of context, these lapses may seem pretty obvious, but believe me, I see them in the manuscripts of very knowledgeable writers all the time. As part of a bigger picture, they're easier to miss.

Just remember, *the point of view is where the camera is and the camera is always somewhere.*

Additional Point of View Exercises:

1. Take a fairy tale (*Cinderella, Little Red Riding Hood, Jack and the Beanstalk*) and write it from the point of view of someone other than the main character. For example, tell Little Red Riding

Hood from the point of view of the grandmother or the wolf.

As a variation of this exercise, imagine an incident such as a car accident, the break-up of a marriage or a closely fought sports event. Then describe that incident from the point of view of two or more people involved. In the instances mentioned, the points of view might be the two drivers of the cars and a passenger, or the husband and wife and child, or various members of the two teams that played.

2. Rewrite a few pages of your novel from the point of view of one of the minor characters.

3. Try telling the story, or part of the story, of your novel aloud (perhaps using your writing group as an audience) in third person, and then in first person.

4. Go back to the last three novels you've read. Identify the points of view. Look at how points of view were combined. Continue to do this as you read more novels. Look for point of view lapses and mid-scene shifts.

5. Take a few pages of writing—either your own or someone else's, published or otherwise—that's written in multiple points of view. Rewrite it in one point of view, either first or third. See how you can convey much of the same information in that one point of view.

CHAPTER FIVE

Words Are All We Have

The Use of Language, Description and Detail

The book that first inspired me to write was George Orwell's *1984*. Early in the novel, a character explains how the government is destroying words. "Don't you see that the whole aim of Newspeak is to narrow the range of thought? In the end we shall make thought-crime nearly impossible because there will be no words to express it.... Every year fewer and fewer words, and the range of consciousness always a little smaller."

This was Orwell's vision of hell on earth. People would be dehumanized through their inability to express themselves. Not having words goes beyond censorship; it becomes the inability to think.

Writers are in the opposite game. We are giving people language, letting them recognize in our words, perhaps, thoughts they haven't been able to express before. Words are our tools. We don't get enough credit for our use of them, because most of the people we know can use words in a serviceable fashion, in conversation or for cute notes excusing their kids from school. Writers use them differently. As Annie Dillard wrote in *The Writing Life*, "The line of words is a miner's pick, a woodcarver's gouge, a surgeon's probe. You wield it, and it digs a path for you to follow."

It's a big responsibility. I like to think of it as a dirty job that it is our privilege to do.

THE BASICS

The Ground Rules of Strong Prose

Precision

Being precise means that you seek to convey as much information in as few words as possible.

I'd be ashamed to tell you how many times in conversation I flounder. "It's just that. . . . What I feel is like. . . ." Finally I beseech the other person, "You know what I mean, don't you?" Sometimes I get a sympathetic nod.

But conversations are not books and your reader is usually not in the same room with you. You can't fall back on such audiovisual aids as getting down on your knees to get your point across. You must rely on your words alone. And you must always remember that the reader only knows what's on the page in front of her.

That doesn't mean that you don't want to create ambiguity or let the reader use her imagination. You do. But when you are describing something, be it a woman's shoe or a dog's snout, the taste of a nectarine or the color of a sapphire, you want to be as specific as possible.

Being precise helps you to show, not tell. Instead of writing, "She had a lovely garden," write, "In her garden, three rosebushes bloomed." Tell us the color. If you can name the variety, so much the better. "Lovely garden" means a lot of different things to a lot of different people, but if you think that the reader will stop to imagine her idea of a lovely garden, think again. That's why the reader is reading your book at that moment, not pottering in her garden. Show us the rosebushes and let the reader decide if that makes for lovely or not.

If you write, "Clara didn't like Walter," you are telling us something. But not much. That's not to say that the sentence "She didn't like him," would never belong in a novel. Far from it. But you will always be looking for ways to increase the utility of your words, the density of them. You will always be looking for ways to say something very exact, something new.

So instead, let's see Walter light a fat cigar and Clara draw back in disgust. Even better, let's see Walter light that fat cigar and Clara draw back. We'll *infer* the disgust. Even this small interaction is more precise—and more interesting—than "Clara didn't like Walter."

You can see from this example how precise prose aids you in characterization. It should help you in everything, because words are your only vehicle as a writer.

These guidelines will further help you in keeping your prose precise:

No clichés. The quickest, most efficient way to undermine the precision of your writing is by using clichés. We live in a cliché-sodden world and it's easy to get seduced.

"I loved her more than life itself."

"He's been around the block a few times."

"I was climbing the walls."

"Time was running out."

You may think you're saying something, but you're not. These phrases have been so used and abused that they mean nothing. You must become highly sensitive to anything that smells faintly of the cliché and not let a single one of them near your prose. Shoot to kill.

Avoid vague words. We talked about these little devils in chapter two. They are words like "horrible," "awful" and "terrible," and they *are* horrible, awful and terrible, because they convey an opinion, but no concrete information.

Most writers understand the ban on clichés, but sometimes they are reluctant to accept it on vague words. These writers may want to write in a conversational tone and, after all, people use words like "good," "great," "nice" and "pretty" in everyday speech. So, they wonder, what's wrong with writing, "I think cats are wonderful," when that's what the writer would say in real life? *Especially* when the book has a first-person narrator?

I like books written in a conversational tone, and I encourage people to write them. In modern times, a conversational tone often expresses the writer's voice most naturally.

But a conversational tone isn't the same as writing the way you would speak. A novel chisels out something much more precise and interesting than daily speech or daily life. You can capture a conversational tone and still use precise language, though. Look back to chapter four where we first discussed the first person: All the samples quoted there, with the exception of Kazuo Ishiguro's *The Remains of the Day* are written in a conversational tone (though some more so than others) but all use very precise language.

Here's an invented example:

> My sister Lois was in a family way. With child. Knocked up. Did I care? Are you serious? But don't be fooled that she was a painter, that she wore that black velvet hat and those baggy pants. Underneath, she was as square as a bathroom tile. After all, who but a complete square would spend Saturday nights doing homework? That's how she got all those good grades.

The tone here is casual, but the information conveyed is specific. *Use all your senses.* Being used to movies and TV, writers tend to describe first what something looks like, and after that, if they get around to it, how it sounds. Don't forget taste, touch and smell. The odor of cinnamon lingering in the hallway. The rough feel of your face after 5 P.M. (men only, we trust). The sawdusty smell of a newly-built house.

When I picked up *1984* I expected a dry diatribe on politics, and the weakest parts of the book are exactly that. What makes the book live, though, are passages of description that sensually detail the bleakness of life under a totalitarian regime. The conversation between Winston and Syme that I quoted earlier takes place over lunch.

> Winston took up his mug of gin, paused for an instant to collect his nerve, and gulped the oily-tasting stuff down. . . . He began swallowing spoonfuls of the stew, which, in among its general sloppiness, had cubes of spongy pinkish stuff which was probably a preparation of meat. . . . From a table to Winston's left, a little behind his back, someone was talking rapidly and continuously, a harsh gabble almost like the quacking of a duck, which pierced the general uproar of the room.

The "harsh gabble almost like the quacking of a duck" is just one more annoying fact of Winston's surroundings, like an itchy sweater on an otherwise irritating day. But it was the "spongy pink stuff" and the "oily gin" that put the fear of socialism in this left-leaning gal.

You can see here how sensual writing—that is, writing that appeals to the senses—can depict a world that is barren just as well as one that is lush. After all, our senses keep working, protesting their deprivation. A lesser writer might have omitted these details and then, when his writing teacher complained, pointed out, "But I want to make the writing dull so that the reader can see how dull Winston's world is." He would succeed only in writing a dull book.

(N.B.: I'm sure if Orwell had lived—*1984* was published posthumously—he would have edited one or both of the "general"'s out of that paragraph.)

Express emotions indirectly. We often start out writing because we want to express emotions that are important to us. We want others to know how we've felt, how we feel. So it's tempting to write about how waves of fear and sorrow washed over Trisha as she looked at her mother in the hospital bed, about how anxiety and pain and agony nearly choked her.

Some writers can get pretty carried away with this. Fear chokes the character, pain marches up her spine, sadness hangs like a cloud—and all in the same compound sentence. Because I so often see waves of emotions crashing over the heads of defenseless characters, I call this "oceans of emotions" writing.

Writing about emotions as separate beings is always problematic. ("Familiarity confronted me." "Self-consciousness nipped at my heels.") The result is at best telling rather than showing; at worst it is melodramatic and trite. The reader can see an insecure writer trying very hard to get something important across.

When you want to convey to the reader the emotions that the character is feeling, look first to the situation you are writing about. Concentrate on the concrete details: In many cases the situation itself will do the work of conveying the emotion. If you describe poor Trisha's mother connected to a number of intrusive tubes, breathing with difficulty, and let Trisha look on—perhaps while remembering briefly and concretely how her mother comforted her after a fall from a bike ("Trisha had cried on the pink cotton of her housedress then, smelling the talcum power her mother used under her arms")—then we will *be* in the situation with Trisha and we'll feel what's she's feeling.

A student of mine was writing about a woman who was having surgery to remove breast tissue after a series of cancer scares. A nurse asks the woman to spend ten minutes in the shower, washing her breasts with antiseptic. The image of a woman engaged in such an intimate act with a part of her body about to be removed haunted me for days and conveyed all the sadness, loneliness and pure terror of the surgery without using the words "sadness," "loneliness" or "terror."

In another manuscript, a young man is in a Nairobi hospital, waiting for news of his friend whom he brought in with chills and fever, and for whose life he fears. After trying to place a long distance call to the friend's father, the young man slides to the floor. There he sits stunned, watching shoes go by. "Dusty brown ones, scuffed white ones that made no sound, leather sandals slapping the tile under black feet. A cane." This simple description makes the situation, and therefore the character's feelings, more real.

Also look at how you can translate what a character is feeling to physical sensations. In a book called *Loss of Flight*, by Sara Vogan, a woman named Katlyn is contemplating breaking off her relationship with her married lover, Royce. "That thought made her teeth feel as if they were loose in her mouth." This is far preferable to, "Thinking of losing Royce made her weak from sadness and despair."

Sometimes a character's feelings will be totally inappropriate to the situation, in which case the situation will not convey the emotion. Still, you as author can convey the emotion without telling us about it. Imagine that you are writing about a positively paranoid young woman. She receives a gift from a co-worker.

> Annabelle looked at the pen-and-pencil set. It was gold and everyone knew that gold brought bad luck. Claire was smiling at her. Annabelle knew why: Because the gold would send out an energy field that would make pimples appear on Annabelle's face.

You have translated Annabelle's emotions—suspicion, anxiety and fear—into the concrete image of what she thinks Claire can do to her.

Sometimes an author *can* successfully give emotions a metaphoric life of their own. The trick is to let the metaphor do the job, and leave the emotion unnamed. I've mentioned that *One Flew Over the Cuckoo's Nest*, Ken Kesey's novel about a mental hospital, is told through the eyes of a paranoid schizophrenic named Chief. Chief talks about a fog machine, clearly a device of his own delusions, which clouds up the wards. The imaginary fog becomes an indicator of his mental state, and a much more accurate, poetic one than it would be if Chief were constantly complaining, "God, I'm depressed today."

But when in doubt, trust the reader to know what to feel.

Use clear sentences. Test out each sentence you write to make certain that you are not creating any unintentional confusion.

"At the end of the day Dr. Schmendrick suggested that Melina write down her thoughts." This sounds as though Dr. Schmendrick *made the suggestion* at the end of the day. Is that what you mean? Or do you mean that he suggested that she write them down regularly at the end of *her* day? If so, you must write, "Dr. Schmendrick suggested that Melina write down her thoughts at the end of the day."

Another example: "I learned this trick from my brother-in-law, which is obviously not for everyone." The trick isn't for everyone, or learning tricks from your brother-in-law isn't for everyone?

"When Fred came to town he was spitting and shooting up horses." He was spitting one minute, then taking aim at the poor beasts the next—or was he actually expectorating four-legged animals?

You know what you mean when you write and sometimes it's difficult to erase your own knowledge and mimic the state of mind of the reader. Try to read your sentences as if you've never seen them before. Don't let them play in your mind like a familiar tune you can hum without paying attention.

Don't ever be lazy about cleaning up confusion when you see it. Even if the reader would easily guess the meaning, such confusion will, at the very least, disrupt the fictional dream. At worst, the reader will have a laugh *at* instead of with you.

I failed to catch such a sentence in *Get That Novel Started!* I wrote, "Often writing instructors will run private groups out of their homes." What I meant was that these instructors would invite students to gather in the instructor's home for purposes of discussing the students' writing. But a reader wrote to me, quoting the sentence and gleefully adding, "I bet they do!" Only then did I realize the other possible interpretation, which was that the same instructor would be *chasing* the group from her home.

If the double meaning is purposeful, it can make your novel richer. In the Henry James story, "Greville Fane," the narrator is reminiscing about a writer of pulp fiction who has just died. This good lady, the deceased writer, had the misguided notion that she could train her son to follow in her footsteps as a novelist, to which end she supported him in extensive travels that would theoretically make him a more perceptive person. Eventually, though, she pays him to do research for her own novels.

> He was paid by the piece: he got so much for a striking character, so much for a pretty name, so much for a plot, so much for an incident, and had so much promised him if he would invent a new crime.
>
> "He *has* invented one," I said, "and he's paid every day of his life."

The "crime" to which the narrator refers is the way the son has exploited the mother. Ah—but is the narrator saying "He *is* paid for it," or "He *has* paid for it"? (Possibly both.)

By the way, writing clear sentences also means that we always know to whom "he" or "she" refers.

Avoid redundancy. Redundancy arises when two or more words give the same information. I picked up my favorite example nearly twenty years ago when I heard a sportscaster say, several times during one football game, "If you look down on the field, Joe, you can visually see. . . . " As opposed to tactilely see?

Other examples:

"The cathedral was a **jewel** of a **gemstone**."

"I was **frightened**, for **fear** that she would see me."

"The one **inviolable** rule that **you can't break** is the curfew."

"The few **remaining** comments I have **left**."

"A psychoanalyst's **rare** pronouncements become weighty from their **infrequency**."

I hope your intelligence won't be insulted by the boldfacing. In all cases, one of the boldfaced terms can be deleted.

Don't forget that redundancy isn't confined to words within the same sentence. In *Get That Novel Started!* I wrote about what I call the "recap sentence," which is a sentence that sums up what's gone before. An example:

Marvin leapt up high the air and clicked his heels. "Hallelujah!" he yelped joyfully. He was happy.

In this case, "He was happy," is not only telling-rather-than-showing, it's redundant.

Minimal Use of Passive Voice

Active voice describes a character taking action. "I walk to the store." "I buy bread." A feeling-state can be an action, too, at least for purposes of active voice. "I love chocolate."

Passive voice describes a character being acted upon. "I *was chased* by a dinosaur." The character is running, but is *being* chased; the dinosaur is doing the acting. "I *was noticed* in the crowd because of my orange houndstooth jacket." The character is being acted upon by the person or persons who notice him.

Passive voice alerts you to its presence by its use of the verb "to be." (You *will be* alerted to the presence of the passive voice by its use of the verb "to be.") There is no passive voice in the sentence, "I love chocolate, but chocolate doesn't love me." Rather, it describes two characters—you and chocolate—acting.

Usually, active is the voice of choice. We discussed at length the importance of characters taking action and this in the sentence-by-sentence way in which they do so. Characters who reveal themselves in passive voice are more passive, less interesting. They may tend to whine. "I was caught by the police." "I was ruled against by the judge." Even when good things happen, they are not responsible, they're just beneficiaries. "I was chosen to be best man." "I was voted the class clown."

Another problem with the passive voice is that we don't always know who is doing the acting. Take an example we used earlier: "I was noticed in the crowd because of my houndstooth jacket." But by whom? By six riot police who dragged you away to imprison you for bad taste? By an impressionable young woman with a weakness for houndstooth? More concise and informative is, "A dark-eyed beauty noticed me in the crowd."

Used consciously and intelligently, passive voice has its place. Certainly a character might use it in dialogue. I've observed to my husband, "The cheese knife was left out." Since passive voice conceals the actor, it's a nice way of saying, "I suspect you of leaving the cheese knife out but I'm merely going to make a neutral observation in hopes that you don't do it again."

You might use passive voice intentionally to create an impersonal atmosphere. "When Ethan entered the party he discovered that it was bigger and noisier than he expected. Dances were being danced, drinks were being guzzled, mysterious cigarettes were being passed around." In this sentence the passive voice, making the revelers anonymous, heightens Ethan's sense of exclusion. But very shortly you will also have to describe the woman doing the Charleston on the table, the wobbly drinkers with their elbows crooked, and the long-haired man licking the cigarette paper, so that we can visualize the action.

When the actor is clear, you can also use passive voice to vary your sentence structure. For example, "When the doctor performed the operation he was assisted by his most promising student," as opposed to, "The doctor performed the operation. His student assisted him." The first is more elegant and there's no doubt about who's doing what, in spite of the use of passive voice.

But always look closely at your use of passive voice, and ask yourself if active would be clearer and/or more lively.

Be Simple and Direct

The writer and teacher Gregg Levoy told me that writers have a patron saint, St. Francis de Sales. It was enough to make me consider Catholicism.

Short of that, though, I can still pass on St. Francis's advice: "Simplicity, simplicity, simplicity."

Often writers try to impress with their grandiose phraseology. But just as the shortest distance between two points is a straight line, usually the best way to communicate a thought is the simplest version. Instead of, "Onto the table he placed his plate," it's preferable to write, "He put the plate on the table."

Another example: "She descended from her vehicle, with the aid of her husband," would probably be better as, "She got out of the car with her husband's help."

Don't write, "he gesticulated," if "he gestured" is just as good. Just write, "The phone rang," instead of "The phone sprang to life."

Those of us who enjoy eighteenth- and nineteenth-century novels might be particularly tempted to mimic the more formal style of that earlier period. If this is appropriate to your material and truly natural for you, fine. But if you are trying to write what sound like elegant sentences because you think that's what writers do, you may be using what Thaisa Frank and Dorothy Wall, in *Finding Your Writer's Voice*, call an "imposter voice." As Frank and Wall put it,

> These imposter voices are essentially "head" voices. They have important uses in other parts of your life. You need them when you're giving a report to the Board of Directors, explaining why your bank balance is wrong, or facing an irate mother-in-law. As the voice that drives your story, though, they'll lead you astray.

When you speak to the Board of Directors, the bank or your mother-in-law, you are often trying to impress or control. In either case you create distance. As a novelist, distance is the last thing you want between yourself and your reader.

That doesn't mean that you have to write like J.D. Salinger or T. Coraghessan Boyle. The point is to find the way of writing that comes from you, uniquely and naturally. Paradoxically, after you wrestle with yourself for years to find that natural way of writing, it will then seem the simplest.

The Sound of Writing

Novels are not read aloud as often as poetry. Perhaps books on tape will change that, when they proliferate to the point where we all prefer to have our books acted out for us while we drive the interstate. But whether or not that happens, still, a well-written book *should* be able to be read aloud and captivate its audience by its sound and rhythm as well as its content.

Every writer has a rhythm. You may have already noticed how, when you put down a book you've been reading for a while, the rhythm of your thoughts is similar to the rhythm of the writer you've been reading. You may even notice that if you start writing immediately after reading, your writing will temporarily mimic the rhythm of that other author. This is why some writers say they don't like to read while they're writing, especially fiction. I can see the danger in reading *at the same time* that you're writing—say, picking up a novel when you take a lunch break—but personally, I don't believe in fiction moratoriums during the period of working on books. If you're a serious writer, you will be working on your fiction almost every day of your life. And if you're a serious writer, you will be reading a lot of fiction. To consign all that fiction reading to the few weeks out of the year that you aren't writing would too severely limit your reading.

In the beginning, it's not bad to experiment with other writer's rhythms anyway—they can help lead you to your own. Finding your personal rhythm as a writer also comes in part from finding your voice, which in turn comes from doing a lot of writing (and rewriting), taking a lot of chances, and being willing to expose yourself. As your voice gets stronger, your rhythm will flow more naturally.

Early in your writing career, though, you'll probably have to consciously vary your sentence structure at times. You'll always be on the lookout for the sing-songey prose that arises from repetitive rhythms.

Let's say you see that you've written, "He went to the bank. He cashed a check. He smiled at the teller." You might revise those three choppy sentences so that they read as one: "He went to the bank where he cashed a check and smiled at the teller."

As an aid to catching awkward or sing-songey prose, practice reading your writing aloud in private. Reading aloud to an audience is an excellent way of discovering where your story drags, where dialogue is stilted, and other problems, as we noted in chapter three. But for the sound of writing, reading aloud by yourself is preferable. You can take your time, repeat passages if necessary, and learn to tune into the rhythm that's yours alone.

Aloud or not, when you re-read, you also want to look for these three problems that will interfere with the smooth sound of your writing:

1. *Rhymes*: "Vaughn yawned." "Ted said." "The man ran." "She was thin to begin with."
2. *Alliterations*: "Shelly shrugged her shoulders." "A big babbling blue brook."

3. *Word repetitions*:

> "He went down to the beach. The beach always calmed him, reminded him of his connection to all life.
>
> "He'd been at the beach for nearly three hours, when, at the end of the beach, he saw a man approaching."

Three sentences, four appearances of the word "beach." I'd try:

> "He went down to the beach. It always calmed him, reminding him of his connection to all life.
>
> "He'd been walking on the sand for three hours when, about twenty yards away, he saw a man approaching."

Don't get paranoid about every repetition of every word, though. If a scene takes place in a winery, the word "wine" will probably appear fairly frequently. Don't perform literary gymnastics to avoid mentioning it twice on the same page by calling it "fruit of the vine" or "nectar of the gods." The point is to learn to listen to your own writing in such a way that you can hear a jarring note, which too many word repetitions can cause.

Rhymes, alliterations and even word repetitions can work if they are part of a larger scheme of word usage in which the rhymes and alliterations are carefully selected, sometimes to demonstrate the skill of the writer. For example, the author might compose entire paragraphs or scenes of sentences that end with words that rhyme with each other, though such extreme techniques are more often found in experimental fiction.

Alliterations, when they occur by choice rather than neglect, can be poetic, as in this verse from the King James Bible (Lamentations 2:11):

> Mine eyes do fail with tears, my bowels are troubled, my liver is poured upon the earth, for the destruction of the daughter of my people; because the children and the sucklings swoon in the streets of the city.

The children and the sucklings swoon in the streets of the city is alliterative and lovely.

James Joyce made purposeful use of alliterations, and in the famous "Molly's soliloquy" from *Ulysses*, he uses the word "yes" repetitively, in such a way that it acquires meaning—it goes from being simple agreement to a magnificent affirmation of life.

Ernest Hemingway was also to repeat words in a way that endowed them with meaning. In "A Clean, Well-Lighted Place" a waiter mentally recites his version of the Lord's Prayer:

> Our nada who art in nada, nada be thy name thy kingdom nada thy will be nada in nada as it is in nada. Give us this nada our daily nada and nada us our nada as we nada our nadas and nada us not into nada but deliver us from nada; pues nada.

"Nada" is the Spanish word for "nothing." The deceptively simple, and very short, story describes an old man who sits drinking in a café while two waiters discuss him: It seems the old man attempted suicide the week before. One waiter sympathizes with the old man's despair; the other dismisses it, because the old man has money. It is the waiter who understands the old man who later recites this bleak prayer. As the waiter repeats the word nada within the prayer, our sense of his fear of death, and of nothingness, accumulates.

Strong Verbs

Another old writing maxim is, "A verb is better than an adjective." This is really a fancy-schmancy way of saying, "Show, don't tell." If you write, "He jogged up the hill," rather than "He was a fast runner," you are more likely to be writing a dramatic scene; either way, the former lets us see the character jogging rather than being told about his abilities.

Similarly, "The author makes a strong connection with the reader," is flatter than "He forges a connection between himself and the reader." Although both sentences have a verb (as do all "complete" sentences), the second version takes the adjective of the first and converts it into a verb that's more specific than "to make."

Never miss an opportunity to use a strong, specific verb. She *stole* the candy. He *kissed* his mother. He *clawed* open the envelope from the FBI. She *excavated* the earrings out of the backseat of the car. Some other verbs I like: *amplify, generate, enchant.*

It's all the rage in modern America to turn nouns into verbs, too. Just be careful to avoid too-trendy usage when you are writing as the author. In dialogue, first-person narration or the character's thoughts, such usage is permissible (where appropriate to reveal character, setting, etc.), but if the author says, "Godfrey was mentoring Fiona," or "Cyril processed the information," that author might sound a bit foolish—at least until the dreadful day when such useage becomes standard.

Qualify Intelligently

Some qualifications only make your writing more vague. "Sort of," "kind of" and "in a way" are among the worst. With qualifications such as these you are saying to the reader, "my description isn't accurate but I won't tell you in what way it's lacking." For example, if you write, "He was sort of nice," it's like saying "Nice doesn't really describe him but that's as close as I can get."

Whenever you see that you've qualified something, ask yourself if the qualification makes what you've written more specific or more vague. Any vague adjectives should be immediately suspect: "He was a wonderful man."

Other qualifiers that often subtract rather than add meaning include *very*, *quite* and *rather*. If he was very tall, then how about telling us he was a giant—or better yet, how about giving us his exact height? If she's rather stingy, then perhaps there's a better word for it: *parsimonious* or *miserly*. Or better yet, tell us how she'll ask friends to give her their unused yogurt coupons.

That doesn't mean that you should slash every qualifying word each time they appear. Sometimes the cadence of the sentence, the tone of the narrator, or even the meaning of the phrase, require them. But be aware of how they can undermine specificity.

Adjectives aren't the same as qualifiers. Qualifiers say something about the intensity of the noun; adjectives speak more to the quality.

Some beginning writers throw on adjectives like ornaments on a Christmas tree, figuring that more is better. This is a sign of insecurity and impatience. The writer just can't wait another sentence before she uses the word "inchoate," so she has to write, "The cake failed to rise and so looked unformed, inchoate." When adjectives are overused, they blur.

But adjectives are still an irreplaceable part of language. We don't all have to write like Hemingway (who along with his skill for word repetitions had a near-miraculous ability to make such vague adjectives as "good" convey meaning). There are adjectives for which there are no substitutes, adjectives that can be used originally and precisely. I had a friend who had a gift for such precise, original adjectives and I've never forgotten some of the things she said to me just in casual conversation. Once I was telling her about breaking up with a boyfriend and she observed, "It's such *primitive* pain." Another time when I told her that I didn't answer the phone when I was writing she agreed, "When you work, you have such *fragile* concentration."

In *1984* Orwell describes Winston Smith tasting coffee with sugar (instead of the usual saccharine) for the first time in years. The coffee has "a *silky* taste." When I read that it struck me as so perfect, that I've never drunk a cup of coffee with sugar in it without thinking of Winston Smith.

Ponder your adjectives and the qualities they imply. *Workmanlike* prose. *Sturdy* prose. *Durable* prose. *Muscular* prose. Adjectives aren't the enemy; sloppily used adjectives are.

Metaphors and Similes

Metaphors and similes add texture and lyricism to your writing. They are where your prose becomes the most like poetry, inviting the reader to go beyond the bare facts of the scene and take playful, imaginative leaps with you. They can accomplish other things as well.

First let's distinguish between metaphors and similes, in junior high English class form: A simile is when something is compared to something else with "like" or "as." "He ate like a pig" is a simile. So is, "Slow as molasses in January."

A metaphor tells us that something *is* something else; the "like" or "as" is implied. "He was a pig." "The moon was a hard-boiled egg in the sky."

Many writers use metaphors and similes sparsely or not at all. Metaphors and similes definitely lend themselves to a more flowery manner of writing. An action novel complete with guns and tanks may not call for many metaphors. It's also a question of style and personal taste.

Metaphors and Similes Can Reveal Character

In dialogue, or in first-person narration, the type of metaphors and similes one uses can say something about where the speaker is from. "The Yankees would be down on me like a duck on a June bug," Rhett Butler says when Scarlett begs him to scare up money to pay the taxes on Tara. We know from that regional simile that Rhett is not a New York stockbroker.

Metaphors and similes can also reveal character in third person. "Her laugh sounded like a machine gun," conveys a hardness about a character that "her laugh sounded like a wind chime" does not. "He was built like an oak tree" and "He was built like a missile" create two different impressions of a character, even though they might roughly describe the same physique. The oak tree evokes sturdiness, longevity; the missile speed, danger.

Metaphors and Similes Can Set a Mood

The writer of historical fiction can reinforce the mood of his setting by using metaphors and similes appropriate to the time in which his novel takes place. Here are four from Donna Gillespie's novel, *The Light Bearer*, set in first-century Rome and Germania: " 'Yes,' she said as breathlessly as a young girl repeating the marriage vows." "He actually seemed drawn to them, like lightning to a tree." "He felt his heart had been mauled by an animal." " 'My shame is a serpent with a hundred heads.' "

Metaphors and Similes Can Foreshadow

Those same metaphors and similes can prepare us for future events. In the middle of a cheerful picnic, with birds chirping in the trees like the Vienna's Boy Choir and the sun warming everyone like a heat lamp, the ants might arrive like a tiny but determined army, alerting us that all will not be well for very long. (This overlaps with mood; setting a dark mood in what should be a happy scene can itself foreshadow later events.)

Metaphor and Simile Warnings

Although I encourage writers to use metaphors and similes freely, I've also had students with a gift for them that needs taming. A metaphor or simile that is too long or convoluted can distract from what's going on in the scene. "I was about to confess my affair to my wife when I saw that she was looking out the window, standing so motionless that she reminded me of a bronze sculpture in a back room in a museum in an obscure town, where no one came to visit except on the occasional holiday." By the time we've finished picturing that museum in that town, we've forgotten all about the husband's affair.

Also, metaphors need to be accurate. "His green eyes widened, like fear held in a glass." One could use "fear held in a glass" as a metaphor, but why would it widen?

And metaphors should actually say something new—in other words, add to our impression of the thing depicted. A student described a broken car window sealed with plastic tape, and then wrote, "The broken window was like an old familiar tear that had been stitched together by hand." There's nothing about an old familiar tear stitched together by hand that really says anything about a taped window.

Don't mix your metaphors. "Two weeks out of the marriage, the true colors of her stepfather burst out as if from a ripened pod." "True colors" is a cliché, but even if it wasn't, colors don't burst out of pods. Maybe: "His true feelings burst out like seeds from a ripened pod."

Another mixed metaphor: "She had a laser-like grasp of the ins and outs of relationships." Lasers don't grasp. Maybe: ". . . laser-like insight into the ins and outs of relationships."

Usually one metaphor or simile is all one sentence can handle unless they are fairly simple and/or all describe one person, place or thing. In *Gone With the Wind*, Melanie Hamilton is described as "simple as earth, as good as bread, as transparent as spring water." These are simply stated attributes of one character. *Snow White's* "skin white as snow, lips red as a rose, hair black as ebony," has a symmetry that makes the description poetic. But "Debbie's house was as messy as a war zone and when people walked in they stared at it, stiff as corpses" is probably too much.

Killer-Diller Details and How to Select Them

There's an expression, "God is in the details," and it applies to nothing more than it does to the writing of fiction. That and to the art of telling good lies. And what is fiction, but the telling of lies?

Well, not exactly, but fiction writing and lying do have something in common. (Picasso said, "Art is a lie that lets us see the truth.") In both cases you are inventing something and trying to make someone believe it. Even when you write about something that "really happened" you will find that making the reader believe it is one of your chief tasks.

A good liar knows that if she really wants her lunch date to believe that she was an hour late because she had a flat tire on the freeway, she had better describe the muscular physique of the AAA man who came to change it.

And as a writer, you know that if you really want the reader to believe he's reading about an African safari, you'd better describe the long purple tongues of the giraffes. You must learn that giraffes have purple tongues, or imagine they do, or remember that detail from your real-life safari or trip to the zoo.

A detail doesn't need to be real in the conventional sense in order to have power. Science fiction and horror writers know very well the power of invented, but authentic, details.

One of the most compelling aspects of Anne Rice's *Interview With the Vampire* is that Rice really makes you believe that vampires exist—and she does so by the exquisite detailing of the way they live (or, we might say, *un*live) and function. She casually dismisses any familiar Hollywood notions or even any traditional ones that don't suit her. "Forget that," she says, "this is the way it is." And then she follows her own rules with a steely consistency.

The science fiction writer has to let us know that the qebor eats yodels and yodels eat mordons in order to establish the food chain on the planet Zeek.

Even historical writers are sometimes called upon to fill gaps that history has left. Some novels will permit this type of invention and some will not. But when you do invent in a historical novel—whether it's to surmise the way that the Mimbres celebrated wedding ceremonies or to re-create dialogue spoken by Charlemagne—do so with authority.

Quality, Not Quantity

When it comes to details, more is not necessarily better. The number of details you need to describe a person or to dramatize an event is a result of several factors. What's your writing style? What's the convention of the genre of writing that you're doing? How unfamiliar or unusual is the situation? (The more unfamiliar, the more details.)

But whether you use many or few, it's still important to choose well, to make your details earn their living by revealing much in few words.

One way to do that is by being specific. We discussed this in the section on prose which, of course, details are part of. "A red scarf" might be fine, but how about a vermilion, crimson or raspberry one? You might get away with "a brand new car," but a 1996 Mercedes 450SL in aubergine is bound to tell us more.

Sometimes a metaphor or simile will make a detail come alive. Anne Tyler, in *Dinner at the Homesick Restaurant* writes of "a spindly, starved cat with a tail as matted as a worn-out bottle-brush." Forever and ever I can perfectly see that cat's tail.

Beyond Blue-Eyed Blondes

Another way to make your details work for you is to go beyond the ordinary and obvious. Say your character is walking into a kitchen. Most kitchens have stoves and refrigerators and to tell us that this kitchen does, too, isn't telling us much. Who cares? In the name of being specific, you might tell us that the kitchen has a restaurant-style oven with a six-burner range top, or an avocado side-opening Frigidaire, and you'd be telling us a lot more. But you might also choose to hone in on what's in this kitchen that is not in the usual kitchen: a bowl of strawberries from the owner's own garden; a child's artwork on the refrigerator (and what is the artwork like?); a manual Smith-Corona typewriter on the Formica table. . . .

It's natural when describing a room or a person to start with the obvious. When describing people, beginning writers usually check off hair and eye color. "She was a redhead with green eyes." If they have any energy left they may get on to general physique and then cite the character's age.

I had a student once whom I suspected of having created a format in her computer for character description. "The thirty-six-year-old brunette mother of two was five-five." "The twenty-five-year-old blonde beauty was five-foot-eight." When I encouraged her to vary the description, she came up with, "At six-four, the hulky forty-year-old had gray hair and blue eyes."

I had a devil of a time breaking her of this habit, which to her seemed efficient, since it covered a character's vital statistics in a few words.

It's true that in real life we often only casually appraise the people we meet. If you tried to remember what the waitress at the coffee shop this morning looked like, you might come up with hair color and approximate height, if that. If you're not "into" houses you might not remember much about your neighbor's living room beyond the relationship of the couch to the wing chair.

So—how many times do I have to remind you that novels aren't life? You have to do more than re-create real-life experience for the reader. You have to make it so that she feels she's living it, too.

The problem with documenting only these obvious (if important) facts about a character or an environment is that they're too easy. Sure, we often want to know what a character's hair and eye color is, or her age and height. But we also want to know what it is about this character, or this couch, or this bowling ball, that is unlike any other person, couch or bowling ball in the universe. We want to see the one loose button on a man's shirt. The graffiti scratched in the wood (and perhaps what it says). The Band-Aids on the fingertips of a nail-biter.

How the Part Becomes the Whole

In Ken Kulhkin's *The Angel Gang*, an old man, Leo, receives a beating at the hands of some thugs. At one point he describes how the thugs cut a slit in Leo's eyelid. When Leo closes his eyes, he can see through his eyelid. The image is horrific, but also very specific and concise. The one detail stands in for the whole beating.

That doesn't necessarily mean that you then eliminate all the rest of the description. The exact number of details you include is a function of your style, the genre, and the content. But one killer-diller detail can have more power than twenty unexceptional ones. Here's one from a student manuscript: "The last Zippo I'd seen had belonged to a Nicaraguan contra who'd engraved it with the slogan, 'There's nothing so sweet as the smell of death in the morning.' "

Another killer-diller detail from a student: "The Lakota Club was, for many years, the site of Lawrence Rockefeller's annual New Year's eggnog party. It was the first invitation Mother didn't receive after the divorce." This details sums up the painful changes of a divorce much better than several pages of moaning and groaning about how ostracized the woman felt.

In Barbara Kingsolver's novel *Animal Dreams*, the narrator describes how her sister, Hallie, is so honest that she would tape dimes to broken parking meters. Says a lot in a few words.

Details as Information

Often the killer-diller detail is an obscure but revealing fact. Oakley Hall points out in *The Art and Craft of Novel Writing* that a detail about how horses eat makes the whole scene in which it appears come "brilliantly to life." In such a case, the detail not only allows us to picture something but to fully believe in it, since only someone who knows a lot about the subject would be able to include that detail.

If you ever saw Billy Crystal and Danny DeVito in the movie *Throw Mama From the Train*, you know what I'm talking about from its opposite. Billy Crystal is a teacher of fiction writing, and in an early scene in the film one of his students has written a story about men on a submarine. She reads with great energy, " 'Dive! Dive!' yelled the captain through the thing. So the man who makes it dive pressed a button or something and it dove. And the enemy was foiled again."

Billy Crystal tactfully points out, "When you write a novel that takes place on a submarine, it's a good idea to know the name of the instrument that the captain speaks through."

Knowing the names of the various equipment on a submarine is a necessary starting point. If the writer here can also provide the slang expression the Navy personnel use, that will be a killer-diller detail.

Erich Maria Remarque provides a killer-diller detail in *All Quiet on the Western Front* when his narrator, Paul, describes how he and his fellow soldiers have learned to bayonet the enemy in the stomach, because the bayonet can get caught in the ribs. This dispassionately delivered piece of information about one-on-one combat throws all of war into relief.

An Excercise for Detail-Spotting

There's a technique for training yourself to produce these killer-diller details. Late in the day, take ten minutes to write down the five most interesting things you observed that day. Make this a rigid habit.

Now, when I say write down what you observed, I don't mean the weighty insights you had while watching the clerk bag your groceries (although you can certainly note those down, too, if you want). I mean the most specific, and sometimes off-beat, details that you see (or hear, or taste, etc). It doesn't have to be an alien who landed at the mall and took your parking space. I'm talking about simple details—but details that you might miss if you weren't paying attention. How *does* the clerk bag the groceries—did he put the bread on the bottom? Did he have any unusual physical features? Did he ask you a too-personal question that made you uncomfortable?

Maybe while walking up and down the aisles at the store you noticed that someone had stuck a package of linguine on top of the canned pineapple. Maybe you overheard a pair of twins fighting over who would get to ride in the cart. Those kind of details are hardly earth-shattering. But they're real, and not immediately obvious, the way that writing, "It was a big, crowded grocery store with Muzak playing," would be. As you learn to add these details judiciously to your scenes, your scenes will become more real.

Think of how, when you travel to a strange place, many things leap out at you, from the signs printed in a foreign language to the smells of unfamiliar spices. You need to become a tourist in your own world, to mine even familiar surroundings for unusual details that would strike someone who's visiting for the first time. Your reader is such a person.

Description That Isn't Boring

Description is an accumulation of details that give us a sensory experience of the environment, be it a landscape, people or objects. Description can come in long or short blocks, or it can be broken up into its component details, and sprinkled throughout a scene.

Since we're novelists, and not screenwriters, we have to do a fair amount of describing. But although description is important, it can also be problematic. Maybe this has happened to you: You take your prized, fresh-minted chapter to your writing group. They read it and complain, "We can't see what's going on. You need more description."

So you take it home, add description, then bring it back. There's a new member in the group. "You don't need all that description," he says. "It's boring."

Ah, the joys of being a writer.

Here's the deal: The reader does need to be able to visualize the scene you have written, to see your characters moving through their world. Yet long passages of description that are pure description can be boring, because there's no inherent conflict.

The secret: Write exactly the amount of description you need and no more. When possible, infuse the description with the conflict that's going on in the story. Then, let the description you write function doubly or triply.

How Much Description Do You Need?

Having told you to write what you need and no more, I'm now going to tell you that I don't know how much you need. Every writer and every book is different. Some writers like to give the reader just enough of the bare facts to keep him from getting lost. Others like to write lavish descriptions of every ball gown. More description isn't necessarily better—but it isn't necessarily worse, either, if the description is well-written and functions in the story.

Keep in mind that in a book that covers territory unfamiliar to the reader, you will generally need more description. If your novel is set during the Revolutionary War we will want to know what kind of shoes the characters are wearing, how much they pay for a horse and how they keep warm in the winter without central heating.

A book about modern life often requires less description because we already know what a McDonald's looks like and how fast the average car can drive. That doesn't mean that you can't use your powers of description to show us ordinary life in a whole new way.

Here's a passage from Sue Miller's novel *The Good Mother*:

> . . . I liked the laundromat—the way it smelled, the rhythmic slosh of the machines, the ticking of buttons, zippers, in the dryers, the odd camaraderie among those placed in life by circumstances which meant that they had to wash their dirty linen in public.
>
> Peculiarly for a Saturday afternoon, the place was nearly

deserted. The long row of gleaming yellow washers sat silent, lids up, open-mouthed. Only my laundry hummed and clicked in two dryers. At the back of the long room, a girl stood folding her wash at a table provided for the purpose, and reading the notices which decorated the wall above it. I looked forward even to my turn at the notices, the ads for empowerment workshops, used furniture, lost dogs.

Most of us have been in laundromats before. But Miller's concise and original description lets us see one again for the first time.

Describe the Environment in a Way Relevant to the Scene
Put yourself in the reader's place for this passage of description:

It was a windswept valley, covered with yellow grass, about four acres. At the north end a grove of shady trees huddled together as if for protection. To the west there was a break in the hills.

The sun was dipping below the mountains. Above it, bands of pale peach and nectarine faded to indigo.

We could go on, but even in these five sentences you may begin to get that old so-what feeling. At least the huddling trees give some sense of foreboding.

But what if instead:

The general surveyed the valley beneath him. The yellow grass bent in the wind. *Good grazing land*, he thought. But there wouldn't be grazing tomorrow when the battle began. The enemy would enter through that break in the hills on the west.

The author might continue to describe the prospective battlefield as the general wonders, where will his troops fall back for cover? Will they be able to charge fast enough up the incline? Or perhaps the general sadly observes how perfect the rich brown soil would be for growing mung beans, or notes the few farmhouses in the distance, now deserted by families who fled the approaching armies. . . .

Even if, in our first example, we knew in advance of the description that there was going to be a battle tomorrow in the valley, you can see how involving character and conflict in a description makes description part of the action.

Increasingly, when I see inert blocks of description, my eye tends to skim down to where I can see the story resume. (Obviously, I only do this when I'm reading for pleasure, not when I look at the manuscript of a student or friend.) I'm sure I've missed some delectable similes and stunningly precise adjectives that way. Unfortunately, I don't think I'm alone in this tendency. But when the description is mingled with story, the reader swallows it like the onion that's ground up in your meat loaf. Doesn't matter if he doesn't like onions.

Sometimes it *will* be enough simply to establish how the environment functions in the story first. Let's say a family has suffered financial reverses and so must sell their big house in the city and move to a little town. Knowing the emotional baggage they bring to this new place will add poignancy to the author's description of it. But even in this case you could juice up long passages of description with reminders of how the place being described could affect the characters. "The house was small, but had lots of closets for a kid to play in." "The library was well-stocked, and Jimmy was a book-lover, although Sarah would just as soon hang off the stone lions in front."

Another technique is to save the description for when you need it. For example, wait until Jimmy has cause to visit the town library before you describe its stone lions and well-stocked shelves. (Sometimes you will describe something in advance for purposes of foreshadowing, but even then it's a good idea if you can weave the person, place or thing being described into the current story.)

Remember that when you nail something down for a long, careful description you create in the reader's mind the expectation that whatever you are describing is important. Don't spend three pages on the layout of the cannery unless someone's going to work there, or get hurt there, or start a strike there. The amount of time you spend describing anything is in direct proportion to its importance in the novel.

Let Description Function in More Than One Way
Description can foreshadow, set a mood and/or reveal character. Look at this description from Robin Cook's *Coma*:

> The pathology lab was in the basement of the main building. Susan descended the stairs and emerged in the middle of a basement corridor which disappeared into utter darkness to the right and twisted out of view to the left. Stark bare lights glowed at intervals of twenty to thirty feet. The light from each bulb met the light from the next in an uneasy penumbra, causing a strange interplay of shadows from the

tangle of pipes along the ceiling. In a vain attempt to provide color to the dim subterranean world, angled stripes of bright orange paint had been painted on the walls.

Have you ever been in a hospital so poorly lit? Neither have I. But in his somewhat crude fashion, Cook is portraying a horror-movie setting. Nothing deadly is going to befall to Susan immediately, but the description effectively creates an expectation that ghoulish happenings are afoot.

For another example, look back to chapter three, to the section on foreshadowing. The passage quoted from *The Great Gatsby* is a model of description that functions not just to let us see the landscape but to prepare us for future events. And in chapter two, we discussed how character can be revealed through physical description.

And Finally, Write for Your Genre

I've already acknowledged that different writers, and different genres of books, call for more or less description. They also call for different kinds. Describe what's important to the genre you're writing in. The readers of a "sex and shopping" Judith Krantz-style novel will be looking for lots and lots of brand names, especially of designer clothes. A sword-and-sorcery novel will require you to describe some magic. The reader of a mystery wants to see police procedure, an autopsy and a murder trial.

And whether your novel takes place in Boston during the Revolutionary War or on Wall Street in 1995, whether you aspire to write the most literary fiction or the most popular (or both), you should always be looking for the killer-diller details that stand in for a half dozen banal ones.

THE FINER POINTS

The Objective Correlative

The term objective correlative was coined by T.S. Eliot in an essay called "Hamlet and His Problems." As with many literary terms, it gets thrown around somewhat loosely. Even so, it's a highly useful concept. Let's define it here as *something in the outer landscape that stands in for something in the inner landscape.* In other words, it is something objective that correlates to something subjective. It can be an object, an action, a series of actions or the weather. It can be anything concrete—that is, anything actually happening in the novel, as opposed to a character's thoughts or the author's metaphor.

A student of mine was writing a manuscript in which a woman, Katie, is participating in a support group for women with cancer. The group meets in the home of the facilitator. Sitting in the living room, Katie's attention wanders to the window where she witnesses a cat stalking, and finally killing, a bird.

The cat stalking the bird is an objective correlative. It stands in for Katie's feelings about her own cancer: that she's being stalked by the disease, which might kill her.

When your writing group is telling you that you need more description, think objective correlatives. Objective correlatives can also help you avoid "oceans of emotion" writing. The drama of the cat stalking the bird conveys Katie's feelings more richly than it would to write, "Katie was depressed and angry about her disease."

Anne Tyler's novel, *Breathing Lessons*, ends with a powerful objective correlative. *Breathing Lessons* is the story of Maggie and Ira Moran, a middle-aged working class couple married for years, whose children are now grown. Maggie is flighty and frumpy, but always compassionate. Ira is her more reserved husband. The book tells the story of their auto trip to the funeral of a friend. But their journey takes them near the home of their granddaughter and former daughter-in-law, from whom they have become estranged. Maggie wants desperately to reunite her son and his ex-wife, so they can all be a family again, but her attempt fails, in part because of Ira himself, who doesn't believe it possible.

Throughout, Tyler closely examines many relationships, especially the misunderstandings that arise in a marriage. In the final scene of the novel, Ira is playing solitaire while Maggie frets about her many attempts at kindness that have ended, somehow, in people getting hurt. She observes of Ira's solitaire game, "He had passed that early, superficial stage when any number of moves seemed possible, and now his choices were narrower and he had to show real skill and judgment."

The game of solitaire is an objective correlative. Watching Ira play, and then reading Tyler's-via-Maggie's perception of it, we see that it stands in for Ira's mental state. His youth was the beginning of the game, when he could have married Maggie, or married someone else, or stayed single. In the middle of the game there are fewer choices. He has to play the hand he dealt himself. Is he going to make the best of it? Does he ever want to sweep the cards from the table?

Unfortunately, looking too closely at an objective correlative is like explaining why a joke is funny. With too much explanation the objective correlative loses its power, which derives from our emotional, rather than our intellectual, response to it. But you can certainly see how transferring these observations about youth, middle-age and marriage to a game of solitaire make the book far less preachy and much more true. That's what art is all about. If I tell you what I think, I'm just boring you with an opinion. But if I weave what I think into an experience, then we'll share that experience, even if we might disagree about how to interpret it.

In the same novel, Anne Tyler uses another, recurring objective correlative. Ira whistles songs that reflect his mental state. "This Old House." "The Wichita Lineman." Even, at the end, a phrase from the Grateful Dead's "Truckin'." It's a very basic, but effective, example of an objective correlative.

Literary fiction in particular thrives on objective correlatives. Take this example from Fenton Johnson's *Scissors, Paper, Rock*. The second chapter (the book functions doubly as a novel and short story collection), tells the story of Elizabeth and Dennis. They were small-town sweethearts: She was the cheerleader, he was the basketball star. After high school Elizabeth left to make her fortune as an actress in Hollywood, while Dennis stayed behind, married another woman, and fathered three children.

Now years later they meet again when Dennis helps Elizabeth cart a tombstone from Philadelphia back to her hometown where it will mark her family's graves. They confess to each other that each has been disappointed with their lives since high school. They make frantic love near a deserted road. But afterwards Dennis realizes, "I thought I was waiting for you. Come to find out I've just been . . . I don't know. Waiting."

At the end of the story, after they stop at a gas station, Dennis joins an informal basketball game. Elizabeth watches. Author Johnson beautifully describes how Dennis executes a perfect basket and how Elizabeth almost involuntarily whistles her admiration.

This final shot of Dennis playing basketball while Elizabeth watches is a rich objective correlative. Are the characters resigned? Are they celebrating what's left of their lives? Or are they trying, once again, to recreate lost glories—him the star, her the cheerleader? The final image of them is open to interpretation and yet tells us so much.

Recently a friend of mine, Rebekah, told me a story about a friend of hers, Gary, who was dying of AIDS. Rebekah was helping Gary prepare to leave the Bay Area; he was going home to spend his final days with his family in another state. Rebekah told me,

"He said he wanted to buy a pair of blue jeans, so we swung by The Gap."

The blue jeans are an objective correlative; they represent everything commonplace that we take for granted when we're healthy and expect to remain so.

Objective correlatives can be difficult to come up with because even more than some other elements of writing, they require a delicate balance between conscious effort and the ability to surrender to unconscious processes. You have to go with what feels right and yet be willing to accept that sometimes what feels right won't be right, that you won't convey what you want and you'll have to go back and change it.

Become aware of objective correlatives in others' writing. Then, over time, you'll be able to look at what you're doing and nudge your own objective correlatives closer to the surface.

REWRITING NOTES

The Process

As you know, I generally encourage writers to concern themselves first of all with getting through a first draft. Far too often I've seen a writer spend two, three or even more years caressing his first fifty pages. It's enough to make him feel as though he'll never finish the book.

Also, if you confine yourself to too small a piece of the novel for too long, you limit the amount of learning you can do to the problems posed by that section. You need to put yourself and your characters into a variety of situations in order to gain mastery over a similar variety of challenges.

As you slog through your first draft, your prose should become stronger of its own accord, *if you are working on it*. That is, you should be constantly asking yourself, "How can I make the scene I'm describing as vivid as possible? Am I using the most specific words I know? Are there any clichés, familiar expressions or vague adjectives I can excise?"

When the time comes to do your second draft, you will be a much better writer. You'll rewrite passage after passage, not minding the effort, happy to watch your own prose in action.

Remember that on your second draft especially, you'll do more than edits—you'll be generating new sentences. Rewriting prose is easier than rewriting plot, because cutting out an adjective doesn't force you to make changes elsewhere in the book the way cutting out a storyline does. Still, you must approach your second draft with an overhaul, rather than a tweak, mentality. That's all the more reason to get that first draft down first. What's the point of polishing a paragraph twenty-eight times when you don't know yet whether the scene in which that paragraph lives will still be in the novel next week?

I'm not advocating any shortcuts here. By the time the book is finished, you will most likely have revised many paragraphs twenty-eight times or more. What I am warning you against is burning yourself out on nitpicky rewrites before you get a chance to look at the big picture. It can especially be a trap for former short story writers or poets who are used to working on much smaller canvasses.

There's another side to this, however. Some writing teachers and books are very good at getting you to freewrite—that is, to let the words pour out of you. Unfortunately, some writers learn how to do this and then start collecting freewritten manuscripts like so many beached whales.

Getting the material on paper is a crucial first step; unless you can do that, you'll have nothing to reshape. But you also have to learn how to revise, which is one of the reasons that there is a special section on rewriting in most of the chapters of this book.

Also, I've occasionally had a student who, while moving forward in her novel, was not improving her prose the way she would like. In such a case I do suggest that the student take some time to polish some sections of her novel as she goes. I noted earlier that rewriting is just as important as writing. At least as much learning takes place in the process. Just as you need to experience what it's like to get a scene down on paper, you need to experience what's it's like to reorganize a paragraph, pull a scene from the mush.

Sometimes, you should rewrite something that you know you're not going to use anyway just for the fun of it. Seriously. See how you can make it more precise, lyrical, moving, concrete. When you do this with something that you know you aren't going to use, you can relax a little more about it.

The Practice

Let's look at a handful of sentences that illustrate some of the problems we've discussed in this chapter.

• "He was a scintillating, bright conversationalist." The adjectives "scintillating" and "bright" aren't identical, but they're similar enough that they detract from, rather than add to, each other.

- "She pushed back her fox-red hair then she tightened the belt of her dove-gray robe." What's particularly awkward here are the two compound adjectives—two animal colors, no less! But if you wrote, "She pushed back her fox-red hair then tightened the belt of her silver robe," the sentence would still be a little sing-songey. There are many ways you could vary it, including, "She pushed back her fox-red hair and then, with a sigh, tightened the belt of her silver robe."

- "He wore baggy khakis." The two short *a* sounds in "baggy" and "khakis" when joined with the very similar glottal letters *g* and *k* call unwanted attention to themselves; the two words almost seem to rhyme. Maybe the khakis can be loose.

- "It was sort of late." "Sort of" makes the sentence more vague. You can write, "It was late," or perhaps tell us exactly what time it was. (Hours and minutes are fine; we don't need to know that it was 9:17:56 P.M.)

- "I felt the unbearable sick feeling of suffering the pain and embarrassment of witnessing someone commit a flagrant *faux pas* from which she couldn't extricate herself." This is a case of an author who really wants to convince us of the pain and embarrassment. The *faux pas* itself should convey that. Try: "I felt embarrassed." Or better yet dramatize the *faux pas* and let the reader feel the embarrassment.

- "He was absolutely, totally terrified." This is telling, not showing. Adding "absolutely" and "totally" won't convince us if we don't believe it already. You may not even have to say that he was terrified if you show him running down the street screaming.

- "The bride was like a single white rose among a profusion of pastel-clad bridesmaids." The metaphor isn't finished. It could be, "A rose among wildflowers" or "A white rose among pink and yellow roses."

- "The alcohol burns as it goes down, leaving claw marks on his throat." A mixed metaphor. In the first part of the sentence the author uses burning as a metaphor for the sensation of drinking alcohol. We use that expression so often that we don't think of it as a metaphor, but it is—otherwise you'd have no esophagus left after taking a shot of whiskey. If the alcohol were compared to a cat (although I don't know why it would be), it could leave claw marks on the character's throat.

- "There was an air of finality in his tone." Under most circumstances this can become, "His tone was final."

- "I'd been in the furnished apartment rental business for a long time, which was how I got to know an executive at Able Furniture, from whom we rented furniture for our furnished units." You guessed it—the word "furniture" and its variations appear too often. How about, "I'd been renting furnished apartments for a long time, which was how I got to know an executive at Able Furniture, with whom we did business."

- "It was thought best to cut funding to the sports program." Passive voice is the possible problem here. What we don't know is, *who* thought it best to cut the funding? Actually, I could hear this as a line of dialogue spoken by a prissy bureaucrat who both enjoys her power and doesn't want to take the rap for what she does. So, if we're not supposed to know who thought it best to cut the funding, OK. Otherwise, tell us.

- "We danced subtly, clearly, yet frenetically." Subtly, clearly and frenetically are good adverbs. But better to see the movements of the characters' arms, legs and heads, the perspiration on their skin, the splinters on their bare feet from dancing on the redwood deck.

- "Nothing feels worse than a leaky roof." It's telling-not-showing, and it's vague. How about, "The first drop that leaks through your roof is an invader, proving that your home isn't safe."

- "He was hitchhiking, wondering if anyone would ever stop while the wind blew in his face." This sounds as though the hitchhiker thinks that passing motorists will be discouraged by the wind. Try: "He was hitchhiking. The wind blew in his face, and he wondered if anyone would ever stop to pick him up."

- "The butterflies in her stomach started churning." A cliché that becomes a mixed metaphor.

- "Rachel nodded her head in agreement." This would probably be better as, "Rachel nodded her head." People rarely nod their heads in disagreement.

Consider each sentence, over and over and over. Make sure you've held it up to the light and examined it closely for cracks.

Study the Rules

If you have a lot of difficulty with basic grammar and punctuation you should take a grammar course at your nearby community college. Often such classes are free. It's worth the investment of your time, because no matter how talented you are, you need to be able to write according to the rules. Get a couple of good style manuals to keep near your desk.

When you know the rules, you can break them all you want, because you'll be breaking them intelligently. This applies to every area of fiction, by the way.

And when you doubt that it's worth all this labor and toil, then think of Cyrano de Bergerac. Cyrano may be a soldier, but he's a poet and playwright first of all, and he says of his own writing,

> When I have made a line that sings itself
> So that I love the sound of it—I pay
> Myself a hundred times.

Additional Exercises (and Advice) for Developing Strong Prose

1. Listen to talk radio for a half hour and see how many clichés you can pick out in the host's, guest's and callers' speech. There are plenty of clichés on television but on radio you can concentrate more easily on the words.

The people who call into talk shows have every right to use clichés, so this isn't a value judgment against them. Clichés are almost everywhere, but one place they shouldn't be is in your novel, and this is a good way for you to practice cliché spotting.

2. Read poetry. Poets use language differently than novelists; often more daringly. Reading poetry you can get a better sense of the possibilities of language in a shorter time. If you don't have a favorite poet, just browse *The New Yorker* on a weekly basis.

3. Write a scene such as a wedding, funeral or trial in which people are feeling strong emotions. Don't use any emotion words (like "she looked pleased" or "he said sadly") at all.

4. There's an object—a dress, a weapon, an appliance, anything—that you want to buy but can't afford. Describe it. (Imagine what you might do to get it.)

5. Describe your favorite painting.

6. Describe a city that you are visiting for the first time.

7. Describe the house or apartment in which you grew up.

8. Learn the names of flowers, trees, animals, makes of cars, aircraft, galaxies, tools, exotic foods, fabrics and anything else you can.

9. You may already be a journal-keeper, and if so, you may find it a good outlet for thoughts and feelings, a safe place to *kvetch* (the Yiddish word for "complain") about your life, especially the burden of being called to be a writer. You may have even fallen into the Journal Pit. This is the name I've given to the phenomenon that occurs when you're writing, but the writing

that you're doing mostly consists of very abstract complaints about the unfairness of life. ("I can't help being like Dad because he was my only role model.")

There's nothing wrong with complaining; I'm making a career of it myself. But in the Pit you are not utilizing the journal as a tool to improve your writing. So instead (or at least, in addition), take just ten minutes a day to use a journal to work on your prose.

In order that you don't sit down at your journal with nothing to write about, keep a list of ideas to get you started. You can begin your list with any or all of the exercises listed above. Many are centered around static description rather than story, but in your journal, let the ideas take you anywhere you want. Add to the list of ideas on the front page of your notebook or in a separate file on your computer, so that you always have a list to refer to.

When you write in your journal, think of yourself as a pianist doing scales, a ballet dancer warming up at the barre. Consciously look upon what you do in this journal as nothing you're going to keep.

10. And be willing to write, write, write and rewrite, rewrite, rewrite. Wrestle your sentences down to the ground; you must be master of each one.

CHAPTER SIX

Style Makes the Novel

THE BASICS

Your Style Is a Four-Piece Band

If the writer's voice is the soul of her writing, then her style is her persona—the made-up face she presents to the reader. Style is not your message, it's how you deliver your message—but it's still part of the package, just as your appearance is part of who you are.

A good singer is good *a cappella*, but you might also want to hear him sing with a band. The novel is the singer and your style is the band.

OK, enough with the metaphors. Style is the personal and idiosyncratic ways in which you combine your words with the conventional accessories of novels: where you choose to end scenes and chapters, whether you like polysyllabic adjectives or none at all.

Always remember that style does not make up for substance. Such jazzy touches as humorous chapter titles and obscure literary epigraphs, when they emerge from and are integrated into the novel itself, can highlight a theme of your work, while just plain adding to the reader's (and your) enjoyment of the novel. But strong characters and a well-structured plot are still the foundation.

Just as your mood may change from day to day and yet you remain the same person, so may your style change from book to book. In fact, style is a more readily altered element of writing than voice, because it is more consciously adopted.

So, with our overview of some of the stylistic devices that novelists adopt, you will be better equipped to find the unique combination of accessories that best express your own writer's personality/

persona. Perhaps it will give you ideas for some entirely new tricks of your own.

No Time Like the Present, or the Past

Most novels are written in the past tense. But the present tense has become more popular in recent years, no doubt influenced by the increasing use of the present tense in short stories.

Perhaps in turn the popularity of the present tense in short stories reflects the greater immediacy of our fast-paced MTV world. But Dickens used the present tense in his novels, so it's not an entirely new device, either.

The question of whether to write your novel in past or present has many components, and once you've made that decision you may find that you still do some mixing of the two tenses. The time line of novels written either in past, present or a combination of tenses can be a tricky one, so let's look at the whole issue step-by-step.

The Past Tense Novel: Where Are They Now?

When we read a novel written in the past tense, we assume that somebody—be it first-person narrator, character described in third-person limited or the omniscient author—is looking back on all that has transpired. And yet, in the majority of novels, we never know where that person is now. So, for example, Nick Carraway tells us, at the end of *The Great Gatsby*, "After Gatsby's death the East was haunted for me . . . I decided to come back home." Written as it is in past tense, we might imagine that Nick is now back home. But who knows? Maybe a month after he returned to the Midwest he decided to become a missionary in China. It doesn't matter, really. Fitzgerald has told us the story that he wanted to tell us, and when it comes to the end, he stops.

Similarly, Tolstoy, writing *War and Peace* in the past tense, followed numerous characters through many years and even more adventures. When he got to the end of the novel, he froze them in the past. We don't know whether Natasha's marriage continued to be happy, or what happened to Prince Andrei's orphaned son when he grew up. Neither does Tolstoy place himself, as omniscient author, in a particular place or time.

Therefore, the typical novel, staying in past tense throughout, assumes an eternal perspective on the events described. (By the way, in a conventional past tense novel, you can write, "Elena was the kind of woman who would always tell the truth," without implying that Elena, wherever she may be, is no longer honest.)

However, some novelists do choose to fix their characters in the point of time and/or place from which they are looking back on the events described in the novel. Holden Caulfield tells us in the opening of *The Catcher in the Rye* that he's now out in California, implying that he's in a mental institution or sanitarium of some kind. Jane Eyre describes to us at the end of *Jane Eyre* the current state of her marriage to Edward Rochester.

When the character of a past tense novel is fixed in time, that time is written about in the present tense, as in this passage from *Jane Eyre*:

> My Edward and I, then, are happy: and the more so, because those we love most are happy likewise. Diana and Mary Rivers are both married: alternately, once every year, they come to see us, and we go to see them.

Another example comes from Scott Smith's novel, *A Simple Plan*. This suspense novel tells the story of two brothers and a friend who find four-and-a-half million dollars in the wreckage of a plane. The narrator is Hank, one of the brothers: On the surface, he's the sensible one of the three, and he proposes a plan that will allow the men each to keep a third of the money. But thread after thread comes loose in the scheme. When it's all unraveled, Hank has murdered several people, including his own brother. And just when Hank and his wife think they may at least have the money to console them, they discover that the bills are in effect marked, and they have to destroy it anyway.

The book is written in past tense. But after Hank burns the cash, he shifts to present tense to set himself in time and to tell us what his life is now:

> After I burned the money, I flushed the ashes down the toilet. I still have the rest of the stuff—the duffel bag and the machete and the ski mask and the sweatshirt, the old woman's purse and jewelry and fur coat, the cashier's watch and wallet and keys. I'd planned to go out into the woods somewhere once the ground thawed and bury it all in a big hole full of lye, but it's been five and a half years now, and I haven't done it yet, so I doubt I ever will.

Notice that the first sentence of this passage is written in the past tense, because Hank is describing an event that occurred five and a half years ago. But the next sentence shifts to present. As we'll see, the present tense can underscore the urgency of a particular passage and in this case it intensifies the bleakness of Hank's present situation—in which he and his wife live with constant guilt—by making it seem as though it can never end.

When you establish a present time for a past-tense novel, you establish a perspective for the characters. We know that Holden Caulfield is still a young man as he tells the story of his adventures—he can't bring the harder outlook of middle age to his tale. And we know that when Jane Eyre recounts the story of her trials and tribulations with Mr. Rochester that she is doing so from the vantage point of a woman who is now happily married to the same Mr. R. Hank, the accountant-turned-murderer of *A Simple Plan*, is looking back on the events from the present hell of his life.

Catching up to the present is a nice realistic touch, but a novel that does not catch up to the present, ending instead entirely in the past, like *The Great Gatsby*, possesses a different kind of truth. It's *history*. We infer that it's all unchangeable. The characters aren't going to go into therapy and come out with a different interpretation of their lives. Fixing the perspective of the novel may leave it more open-ended (which may be what you want), and it may explain the characters' take on events.

There's a practical side to the literary choice as well: It's important to keep firmly in your own mind what the present time of the novel is. *Anything that's still true in the present of the novel is written in present tense.*

Early in *Jane Eyre*, Jane describes the death of her schoolmate, Helen, from consumption. The description, like most of the rest of the novel, is written in past tense. But Brontë, as Jane, then adds:

> [Helen's] grave is in Brocklebridge Churchyard: for fifteen years after her death it was only covered by a grassy mound; but now a gray marble tablet marks the spot, inscribed with her name, and the word "*Resurgam.*"

The present time of *Jane Eyre* is at the point at which she has been married to Mr. Rochester for ten years. When Jane describes the gray marble tablet that marks her friend's grave (which we infer Jane herself has placed there), it is a fact of that present, and described in that tense.

Note that in either past or present tense, Jane's description of Helen's grave also works as foreshadowing. In retrospect it promises us that Jane prospered adequately to afford to provide her friend with this dignity of a tombstone, although when we read it we can't know that for sure; perhaps the benefactor will turn out to be someone else.

Similarly, Scott Smith in *A Simple Plan* foreshadows in present tense, as in this passage from early in the novel:

> I can look back now and say that in many ways this was the absolute apogee of my life, the point to which everything before led upward and from which everything after fell away.

Sue Grafton wrote her early alphabet mysteries as if they were reports of a case that private detective Kinsey Millhone has just worked on. This is one of the conventions Grafton creates for her novels; in actuality, the reports wouldn't be that long nor that detailed, and they wouldn't be as personal or as dramatized. But the point here is that Grafton has fixed a point in time, very soon after the close of the case, in which the book is supposedly being written. She often makes present-time statements about herself, such as this one from *E is for Evidence*:

> Anyone who knows me will tell you that I treasure my unmarried state. I'm female, twice divorced, no kids, and no close family ties. I'm a private detective by trade. Usually I'm perfectly content to do what I do.

Although the novel is primarily written in past tense, Kinsey can make these present tense statements about herself because at the time of the writing of the novel, shortly after the close of the case, they are still true.

Sue Miller's *The Good Mother* is another past tense novel that catches up the present. *The Good Mother* is the story of a woman, Anna, who loses her daughter in a custody battle after her ex-husband discovers what he believes are sexual improprieties on the part of Anna's boyfriend. It's a rich book that deals not only with the lives of the characters but with society's continuing double-standard for men and women—that the heroine's name is Anna (as in *Anna Karenina*) is no coincidence. At the end of the book Anna describes her life without her daughter in the present tense. As with *A Simple Plan*, this present tense description intensifies the poignance of the ending: We have no reason to believe that conditions will improve for Anna, although we certainly hope they do.

The Present-Tense Novel

When a novel is written in the present tense, we read it as though we are living it, as though the action is unfolding before our eyes.

> They're out there.
>
> Black boys in white suits up before me to commit sex acts in the hall and get it mopped up before I can catch them.
>
> They're mopping when I come out the dorm, all three of them sulky and hating everything, the time of day, the place they're at here, the people they got to work around. When they hate like this, better if they don't see me.
>
> —Ken Kesey, *One Flew Over the Cuckoo's Nest*

Another example:

> "You screwed up."
>
> You nod. It's true. In this case, however, honesty doesn't make you feel a whole lot better. You're having trouble meeting her glare.
>
> "May I be so bold as to ask for a little elaboration? Really, I'm interested."
>
> Sarcasm now.
>
> "Just *how* did you screw up exactly?"
>
> More ways than you can say.
>
> "Well?"
>
> You're already gone. You're out the window with the pigeons. You try to alleviate the terror by thinking how ridiculous her French braids look, like spinnakers on a tugboat.
>
> —Jay McInerney, *Bright Lights, Big City*

You can see the advantage of the present tense. A novel written in the present simulates real experience in a way that a novel written in the past does not. A novel written in the past is more like hearing a story than living that story.

So why isn't every novel written in the present tense? First of all, because the present tense raises technical problems that the past tense doesn't. It's more difficult to narrate (that is, compress time), to foreshadow and to shift among time frames when using the present tense. We'll look at all these problems (and how best to deal with them) in separate sections.

A related technical problem is that in the present tense, the writer theoretically is limited to revealing information as the characters experience it. In other words, in the present you can't as easily write: "A strange woman enters the room. Her name is Darla," unless the character already knows that the woman's name is Darla. Perhaps as the present tense becomes more common in longer fiction, the conventions of the novel will stretch to include such statements, but they remain somewhat awkward today.

Secondly, the past tense has a moral and intellectual authority that the present tense lacks, because it implies that an author or character is looking back on events, interpreting them and selecting what's important for us to know.

By contrast, the present has a more superficial quality. Although in both cases there is a writer behind the words, who should be carefully choosing what to put in and what to leave out, nevertheless in its simulation of reality the present tense makes it more difficult to bring the same depth of insight to the action of the novel.

In the previous section, I wrote about the subtle difference that arises between a past tense novel in which the characters are looking back from an eternal perspective and a novel in which their perspective is fixed at a definite time. The difference between a past tense novel and one written in the present is far more dramatic. The characters have *no* perspective as yet; they are living the events they recount.

Let's look at *Bright Lights, Big City*, just quoted, which is a novel I admire. It describes the adventures of a narrator we know as "You," who in the aftermath of his mother's death and his wife's desertion gets caught up in the yuppie drug scene of Manhattan in the 1980s. The book is suited to the present tense for reasons we'll discuss—it's literary and small in scope. McInerney writes in a wry tone that's both humorous and insightful. Yet he can't take his character much beyond the present circumstances of his life. In *Bright Lights, Big City*, the present tense increases our experience of sharing "You"'s confusion, anxiety and despair, but it gives McInerney little opportunity to interpret those experiences for us.

By interpreting experiences, I'm not talking about ponderous statements along the lines of, "Only now that I've been in a twelve-step program and turned my addiction over to a higher power do I realize what a fool I was." I'm talking about the author's tone, and the perspective of the characters. As critic Ben Yagoda, in the *New York Times Book Review*, wrote, "To describe an event in the past tense means taking a kind of responsibility for it."

Yagoda also suggests that the current popularity of the present tense comes from the influence, on our and successive generations, of movies and television. "You need only read a film treatment (a literary form always composed in the present) to realize that a key influence on this school has been the movies. The present tense lends itself to dialogue, to scenes, to the impartial observation of detail, and not to Henry James style exegesis—circumstances not lost on a generation of authors that has spent more time looking at screens than pages."

This is fine. We've discussed the influence of the screen on many aspects of the novel. But don't let that influence cause you to make the choice without thinking. I had a student who was writing a novel in the present tense, even though it seemed to all of us in the class to belong in the past. He insisted that he had tried to write the novel in past tense, but that it never seemed natural. He just about had me convinced when he let it slip that he had been a screenwriter for some years before trying his hand at a novel. The habit of writing in the present was hard to shake.

Candidates for a Present-Tense Novel

There are two types of novels that are particularly good candidates for the present tense.

Certain literary novels. Especially closely observed literary novels which are fairly limited in scope. "Closely observed" (a term beloved by book reviewers) means, more or less, that the writer is working small, examining the subtle nuances of human relationships and feelings (though always showing, not telling). By "limited in scope" I mean that a book is short (or at least, not terribly long), with a smaller rather than large cast of characters, and covers a relatively briefer rather than longer period of time—say, a year or less, as opposed to forty.

There's no limit to the number of characters you can write about in a present tense novel, any more than there is a maximum period of time that it can cover; I'm just saying that scope is one of the factors you weigh. A short novel, with few characters, that examines those characters' relationships and doesn't cover a long period of time, will not suffer as much from the limitations that the present tense can impose. Meanwhile, in the present tense, it's natural to bring the camera very close in, to look at the pores on people's skins if necessary. The craft of the literary writer is closer to that of the poet or short storyist than the craft of the pop fiction writer; the currency of the literary novel is often minute experiences, and daily transactions in commonplace settings.

Bright Lights, Big City fulfills these requirements, as does Alice Hoffman's *At Risk* and Sue Miller's *For Love* (although a bit longer);

all are written in present tense. That doesn't mean that all literary novels of this type belong in present tense, although certainly many more of them are written that way today.

Special circumstances. The other type of novel that lends itself well to the present tense is actually any novel that will benefit from the present because of its particular subject matter, setting or the consciousness narrating it. Let me illustrate.

Erich Maria Remarque's *All Quiet on the Western Front* is a novel about World War I, from the point of view of a German soldier, Paul. Paul describes many battle scenes and other situations in which the stakes are life and death, such as scrounging for food. This is a case in which the present tense works because of the setting: The immediacy of the action is heightened. An added benefit is that, written in the present tense, it reads like the diary of a soldier. The present also increases the suspense as to the outcome: Will Paul survive the war?

Ken Kesey's *One Flew Over the Cuckoo's Nest* is the story of a mentally ill man, known as Chief, confined to an institution. The first half or so is written in present tense. We might imagine that Chief doesn't have the mental capacity to tell a story from the past; this is an example of how the consciousness narrating the book lends itself to the present. Note, too, that as the book progresses, and MacMurphy, the newcomer to the ward, helps Chief recover his own ego strength, the past tense takes over.

I wrote my first published novel, *Extraordinary Means*, in the present tense, the only thing I've ever written that way. It began spontaneously, but before I was very deeply into the novel I realized why I was doing it. *Extraordinary Means* is a novel about a young woman in an irreversible coma; however, her consciousness is still alive, floating first near her body and later wherever she wants to go. I thought this worked because the reader doesn't know, and doesn't want to know, how or if Melissa survives this novel. Does she return to her body, die or continue this way? Sure, there might be some kind of survival after death and maybe they even have word processors in heaven (being *without* a word processor would be my idea of hell). Still, I thought that the past tense would not only remove some of the suspense around the issue, but that also, her unusual state of being, which Melissa continually discovers new aspects of, was made more dramatic in the present.

My editor—correctly—observed that all novels raise that question of where-are-they-now, and that the conventions of novel writing allow even for a deceased first-person narrator to look back on her past, without the author having to promise anyone an afterlife. Admittedly, I could have done it that way—it would be nice if there were absolute rules, but there aren't.

Other situations that might lend themselves naturally to the present include: a novel set in a hospital emergency room; a courtroom drama, if it's highly fictionalized (real-life trials are agonizingly slow); and certain types of thrillers, say where a bomb squad is constantly rushing to defuse contraptions that would destroy major American cities. In short, any situations in which events are fast-moving.

As with literary novels, I don't mean to suggest that every novel that fits into one of the above categories needs to be written in present tense; rather, these are cases where the benefits may outweigh the burdens.

Narrating in Past and Present Tense

Narration is any section of your novel that compresses time, as defined in chapter one. I've said there that scenes are preferable to narration when possible, but narration is also indispensable to you as a writer, because it allows you to summarize events that don't deserve a scene.

In a past tense novel, narration is generally also in the past or the conditional tense, as illustrated by the example from chapter two:

> The year passed slowly for Ellen. She particularly hated the harsh Minnesota winter weather, unused to serious winters as she was. She didn't drive and was often stuck at home. So she would pass the afternoon writing to her dear friend Paula in Dallas.

The year passed slowly is the past tense. There was one year and it passed slowly. But when you are describing habitual behavior, you often use the conditional tense, as in the last sentence here: *So she* would *pass the afternoon writing to her dear friend Paula in Dallas.*

When you write a novel in the present tense, you must narrate in present tense as well. (You might include narration as part of a flashback in the past tense, but any part of the story unfolding in the present will be in present.) Therefore, you lose the opportunity to distinguish between a one-time occurrence and habitual behavior, at least in your use of tenses. While habitual action in the past tense becomes the conditional tense, habitual action in the present is the same: the present.

The year passes slowly for Ellen. She particularly hates the harsh Minnesota winter weather, unused to serious winters as she is. She doesn't drive and is often stuck at home. So she passes the afternoon writing to her dear friend Paula in Dallas.

In this passage, it is somewhat unclear whether Ellen is passing one or many afternoons writing to Paula. Of course, you're a writer and you're smart. You know to write, "She passes many afternoons writing to her dear friend Paula in Dallas." Even if you just wrote, "She passes afternoon*s* writing to her dear friend Paula in Dallas" you will make it clearer.

The same opportunities will exist in any present tense narration. Look at this passage in the past:

For six months, my daughter Leah was sick. At night she would ask me to get in bed with her and I did, telling her stories for hours on end. Finally she began to get well.

If you rewrote it simply changing the tense, it would look like this:

For six months, my daughter Leah is sick. At night she asks ~~ask~~ me to get in bed with her and I do, telling her stories for hours on end. Finally she begins to get well.

By simply changing the tenses, you have created confusion as to whether Mom tells Leah stories on one night or over the course of many nights. So you instead you might write:

For six months, my daughter Leah is sick. Every night she wants me to get in bed with her and I do, telling her stories for hours on end. Finally she begins to get well.

The simple change from "At night" to "Every night" eliminates the confusion. If you are aware of the possibility of confusion, you can avoid creating it. The fact remains, though, that you lose a tense, one that would further clarify the action.

The above examples also give a taste of how compressing time in general is more difficult in present tense. "For six months, Leah is sick," sounds slightly ridiculous, not to put too fine a point on it. Six months is a fairly long time. To look back on six months and condense them is one thing—in retrospect, certain periods of our lives often seem quite fleeting, sometimes because we want it that way. The night you spent in jail, the day you gave birth, your four years of graduate school, can all be reduced to a page. But to summarize those same periods in the present is another matter— it supposes that you can speed up that time at will. Many of us have spent six months that we *wanted* to speed up—but then we were all the more aware of how slowly the time actually passed. The present tense is good at conveying the way we really live our lives, on a moment-to-moment basis; less effective in spanning the years.

Once again, the conventions of novel writing allow you to take many liberties with so-called reality, and narrating in present tense is one of those liberties. If you are writing a novel that screams for present tense, don't junk the present simply because there are a few passages of narration. But do keep in mind that a novel that relies more heavily on narration is a less likely candidate for the present. And also keep very much in mind the reality you do create when you compress time. For example, instead of writing, "The year passes slowly," it might be preferable to write, "The year *is passing* slowly."

Flashbacks in Past and Present

I don't like a certain kind of flashback, which is the kind of flashback that exists solely to characterize, and therefore replaces dramatic action and/or just weighs down the novel. ("Flashback" is a term used loosely to refer to any section that takes place before the main action of the novel.) However, the uses of moving back and forth in time are many, and the novel would be a poorer thing indeed if authors could only tell their stories chronologically.

Let's say that in the beginning of your novel a woman returns to her home town after an absence of many years, during which time she's achieved fame as an actress. Now she's coming back to get revenge on the small-town folk who treated her badly when she was growing up as a funny-looking kid from a poor family. You plan to write several flashbacks to dramatize this ill-treatment. These scenes will certainly characterize the people involved, but they are also important to the plot, because they will each contain a secret about one of them that the main character will in turn reveal in the present time when she returns to the town, and which will then have an effect on other characters. (You could also write the same novel chronologically, beginning with the woman's childhood, but our way is faster-paced and more suspenseful, at least given the facts here.)

This is how it would work:

Eileen pulled her Jaguar over when she saw Mrs. Johnson wave. "Well, hi, there!" Mrs. Johnson smiled, coming up to Eileen's open window. "Welcome home, Movie Star!"

Eileen smiled back. But she was thinking, *Don't think that I've forgotten, Martha Johnson!*

Fifteen years before, Eileen had arrived at Mrs. Johnson's house to babysit her two children. Mrs. Johnson had answered the door in her new Christian Dior evening gown.

"You're late!" Mrs. Johnson had exclaimed.

"I don't think so," Eileen replied, looking at her watch. "Didn't you say six o'clock?"

"I most certainly did not! I said five."

Eileen knew that Mrs. Johnson had said six, but she knew better than to argue.

"Well, come inside anyway." Mrs. Johnson flounced into the living room. "You've ruined my evening, but there's no help for it now."

And so on. What you've done, then, is establish that you are going into a flashback by using the past perfect tense (Eileen *had* arrived, Mrs. Johnson *had* exclaimed) for two or three sentences, and then, once the time frame is clear, you started using simple past tense again. It isn't necessary to use the past perfect throughout the scene.

Look at how Fitzgerald does it in *The Great Gatsby*:

> . . . One autumn night, five years before, they had been walking down the street when the leaves were falling, and they came to a place where there were no trees and the sidewalk was white with moonlight. They stopped here and turned toward each other.

In this passage Fitzgerald uses the past perfect once ("they *had* been walking") and then returns to the simple past tense.

Sometimes it isn't necessary to use the past perfect at all. Let's say you're writing a murder mystery. The only witness has amnesia. Near the end, with the help of a compassionate psychoanalyst, she retrieves her memory. You decide to put what she remembers from the night of the murder in a scene. This is how it might look:

> Dr. Schmendrick looked deeply into her eyes. Carla felt light, almost transparent. She kept staring back at Dr. Schmendrick. Suddenly she remembered it all.

(scene break)

The night of the murder, a noise woke her up. She lay in the darkness, listening to her heart beat. She thought she heard footsteps downstairs, in the living room. Had someone broken in?

In the above case the time frame is clear, obviating the need for the past perfect.

Going into a flashback in a present tense novel is pretty straight-forward. Just use the past tense. This is how Remarque does it in *All Quiet on the Western Front*:

> Meanwhile Haie sits down beside us He winks at me and rubs his paws thoughtfully. We once spent the finest day of our army-life together—the day before we left for the front. We had been allotted to one of the recently formed regiments, but were first to be sent back for equipment to the garrison, not to the reinforcement-depot, of course, but to another barracks. We were due to leave next morning early. In the evening we prepared ourselves to square accounts with Himmelstoss.

This is arguably one advantage a present tense novel can have over a past tense one: a flashback is clearly a flashback.

Foreshadowing in Past and Present

Foreshadowing is much easier in a past-tense novel than in a present-tense one. In the past tense you can also move into the future, because the future is still the past. OK, let's try that again. Suppose your novel is set in 1954, and tells the story of a woman who marries a wealthy man whom she doesn't love in order to save her family from poverty. In the novel, you may occasionally want to use what I've called blatant foreshadowing by writing things like, "For the rest of her life, Delilah would be sorry she had uttered those fateful words." "And when her daughter got married, ten years later, Delilah looked back and knew that this was the night she could have made it all come out differently between them." Well, ten years later is only 1964, so it's still the past.

A contemporary novel can also move into the future—say, when a novel set in 1995 makes a statement about the characters ten years later. At least in the past tense, this carries the weight of authority.

In a present tense novel, however, no matter what year in which it is taking place, you can't use such blatant foreshadowing, because you will have to use the future tense. Oh, sure you can *do* it—but just not to the same effect. Going back to our original example, you'd be writing, "And when her daughter gets married, ten years from now, Delilah will look back and know that this was the night she could have made it all come out differently between them." The foreshadowing then takes on a mystical quality; someone is foreseeing the future.

Alice Adams wrote a novel called *Listening to Billie* using a mix of past and present tense. In this scene, one of the central characters, Daria, is talking to her niece, Catherine, who is pregnant out of wedlock:

> It is during this conversation that I realize that eventually, somehow, I will be the one to get Catherine's child. Not as my own; she would never give it to me, not stubborn Catherine (nor would Smith ever allow me to adopt a child). But I am sure that it will occur to everyone as a good idea, and in an interested way I will watch to see how this comes about.

And we'll watch with interest, too. This passage is foreshadowing, because it prepares us for events to follow. But it doesn't have the authority that foreshadowing has in past tense—it may or may not come true.

Novels With Stories in More Than One Time Frame

Some ambitious novels have stories that unfold in different time frames. This is something completely different from a novel weighed down by flashbacks—it's a novel with stories in two (or even more) different times that are, or at least should be, integrated in some way.

Fannie Flagg's *Fried Green Tomatoes at the Whistle Stop Café* is a fine example. One story begins in 1985; the two central figures are the elderly Ninny Threadgoode and Evelyn Couch, a middle-aged woman who already feels her life is over. Evelyn meets Ninny when she goes to a nursing home in Birmingham, Alabama, to visit her mother-in-law, and Ninny is soon telling Evelyn all about the people with whom she spent her life in nearby Whistle Stop. We hear some of this in Ninny's own words, but most of it is dramatized for us in scenes that take place beginning as early as 1929.

Ninny's stories of the people of Whistle Stop, and Evelyn's relationship with her, inspire Evelyn to re-evaluate her life and then to change it. The book is quite well-structured and a large cast of characters stay happily clear in our minds. However, Flagg also wisely labels each chapter with the month, day and year in which it is taking place (i.e., "June 24, 1936"), often a good idea in a novel with so many time shifts. It's particularly important in this book because, even within the separate stories, the unfolding of *Fried Green Tomatoes at the Whistle Stop Café* isn't entirely chronological. For example, one of the very late chapters in the past-time story of the Whistle Stop characters (when most of that story is taking place in the late 1960s) goes back to 1930 to explain how the murder of Frank Bennett actually took place, a murder that has thus far gone unexplained. Holding off that explanation scene creates a lot of suspense, but it's also important that we don't get confused as to when the many events of the novel are taking place.

Flagg chose to write *Fried Green Tomatoes at the Whistle Stop Café* entirely in past tense, of which choice (if my opinion matters) I heartily approve. But this type of novel can also lend itself to a combination of present and past. For example, a student of mine was writing a captivating novel about a modern woman taking a camping trip with her husband in an attempt to save their crumbling marriage. The trip itself turns out to be the last excursion they'll ever take together: The marriage disintegrates before our eyes.

While confronting the end of the relationship in this way, the woman at the same time becomes preoccupied with the notion that she may have lived a former life as a pioneer woman, and traveled by covered wagon across the country. Parts of the novel tell the story of the pioneer woman fighting the elements and the prejudices of her time, and other parts tell the story of the modern woman struggling to erect a tent and cook in the outdoors while arguing with her husband.

My student was writing the pioneer woman's story in past tense and the story of the modern woman in the present, which worked for two reasons. First of all, it made sense chronologically: We're living in modern times, but no longer in pioneer times. Second, the modern story involved only a few characters and was more literary in style, while the historical story was broader in scope, covering more time and including more people.

Using the Present Tense in a Past-Tense Novel

You can write a novel in past tense and still use the present tense in certain scenes, or parts of scenes. The temporary use of the present tense can underscore the immediacy or importance of the action.

My favorite example of the use of present tense in a past tense novel is from Charles Dickens's *A Tale of Two Cities*. The novel is set in France and England during the time of the French Reign of Terror, and tells the story of Charles Darnay and Sydney Carton, who both love beautiful Lucie Manette. Sydney, who lives a dissipated life, never really has much of a chance next to upright Charles, but in a moment of sentimental foreshadowing, Sydney promises Lucie that he would "embrace any sacrifice for you and for those dear to you."

Lucie marries Charles who, it turns out, is actually a French nobleman. When Charles returns to France to set right one of the wrongs of his family, he's imprisoned and sentenced to death. At the last moment, Sydney fulfills his promise to Lucie by trading places with the imprisoned Charles, so that he can go to the guillotine in his stead.

The book is written for the most part in the past tense. But the final chapter begins, "Along the Paris streets, the death-carts rumble, hollow and harsh. Six tumbrils carry the day's wine to La Guillotine."

Sydney Carton is riding to his death. And the scene is more dramatic, intense, in the present. The entire novel written in the present would have been extremely problematic, especially as *A Tale of Two Cities* is an historical novel—but the fact that the novel itself is rendered in the past makes the shift all the more emphatic.

As Carton climbs the scaffold he has a vision of what will follow: how Lucie and Charles will prosper, while always honoring his memory, and name a son for him who in turn will prosper and have a son also named for him. This prophecy is written in the present tense—even when a character is granted a vision, the future tense is awkward, though usable—but of course is set in the future. Since the novel *is* historical, Dickens could have shifted back to past tense and described all that followed in the past tense, but located in the mind of Sydney Carton it takes on added meaning as the mercy of God who gives him this knowledge in his final hour.

Another example of the transient use of the present tense comes from a student manuscript. In this scene a young man has broken into an animal shelter with the goal of liberating a dog that is scheduled to be put to sleep.

> The room smelled of disinfectant. Glass-doored cabinets lined the walls; locked within were vials and syringes and

lengths of surgical rubber hose. The cocker spaniel whimpered piteously. In the center of the room was a small stainless steel table with restraining straps that hung limply on either side.

Softly now. The cocker spaniel whimpers in his cage. On the corner of the table and on the floor beneath there are fragments of what Elliot now knows to be dog biscuits. In the corner stands a container, like a large square rubber garbage can. But the lid is secured fast with heavy brass latches. A soft and final sigh of resignation from the spaniel—he lies quietly. Elliot is drawn to the container. All of his instincts tell him not to open it. But a deeper necessity demands it of him. Slowly, with the caution of a diamond cutter, he begins to open the latches. He fingers tremble and beads of sweat form on his forehead. *Click!* The latches release. *Click!* A harsh sound like a revolver being cocked into action. The trembling of his fingers has worked its way up his arms and into his shoulders and chest. His mouth is very dry now and he pants, like a thirsty dog. The cocker spaniel stirs again.

The present tense (combined with short, incomplete sentences) increases the immediacy of the scene. The author can stay in present until the end of the scene, or he can begin a new paragraph back in the past tense. ("Later, what Elliot remembered most was the smell of feces. . . .")

The scene need not be very dramatic in itself to justify the use of present tense. Charlotte Brontë occasionally used the present tense in *Jane Eyre*:

> And where is Mr. Rochester?
>
> He comes in last; I am not looking at the arch, yet I see him enter. I try to concentrate my attention on those netting-needles, on the meshes of the purse I am forming—I wish to think only of the work in my hands, to see only the silver beads and silk threads that lie in my lap. . . .
>
> Coffee is handed. The ladies, since the gentlemen entered, have become lively as larks; conversation waxes brisk and merry. Colonel Dent and Mr. Eshton argue on politics; their wives listen. The two proud dowagers, Lady Lynn and Lady Ingram, confabulate together.

An ordinary event, but the present tense emphasizes how high the stakes are for Jane: She's in love with her master, Mr. Rochester, but as governess to his ward, she's forced to witness this social occasion as an outsider.

You can also use the present tense to distinguish the material described from ordinary reality. For example, you might use present tense when a character is dreaming, drunk, under hypnosis or imagining events.

Dickens's unfinished novel, *The Mystery of Edwin Drood*, alternates sections in past and present tense throughout. But of interest to us is the opening, which is a character's opium dream, described in present tense. (Dreams should be used quite sparingly in novels, but that's another story.)

And here is a passage from a student manuscript, using the attributive point of view, in which a man is imagining the park bench on which his parents met:

> I can see it the way my mother always described it. So we can assume the bench, the sunshine, the cluster of pigeons at her feet.
>
> He offers her a cigarette and she refuses. He lights one for himself with long brown fingers that tremble.
>
> "How old are you?' he asks suddenly.
>
> "How old do you think I am?"

The scene continues with another page of dialogue, with description in present tense. When the narrator first injects his own voice again, it is at the beginning of a new paragraph, and he once again is interpreting these events in the past tense. "That afternoon on the bench was probably the one and only time they didn't fight."

Writing certain scenes in present tense can be extremely effective. Do make the shifts conscientiously, though. There's no rule about exactly when or how, just be aware of when you're doing it and why. I've seen a few manuscripts that went back and forth in the middle of sentences, sometimes several times within a paragraph. The result was a confusing mess.

THE FINER POINTS

The Long and the Short of Sentences, Paragraphs, Scenes and Chapters:

Sentences

Sentence length and style significantly affects the atmosphere you create. Short sentences may make a work more accessible, or indicate a simpler, less-educated narrator (or that we're in the head of same in third person). Long sentences create a more formal tone (think of Henry James).

Faulkner wrote pages-long sentences (a bit intimidating); Hemingway wrote short ones (sometimes). Some writers use incomplete sentences to create atmosphere. Look at this description from a student manuscript:

> She walks through the wood. Light breeze and many leaves. Crunching under her feet. She stops. Lost. Or maybe just wants to be.

In this case, short incomplete sentences increase the sense of disorientation. You can also join complete sentences (or what could be complete sentences) with conjunctives to create a different mood.

> I could hear the man coming faster behind me and I ran faster, too, because the cabin was only a mile ahead and maybe I could get there and be safe before he caught me and then I got a stitch in my side and I thought that if I could only rest for a minute then I'd be OK but I was afraid to stop, because I was sure that the man had a gun and that he might use it if I let him get within shooting range so I kept running even though the pain was spreading. . . .

(As an exercise, try rewriting the above in present tense.)

The *ands* in this passage, taking the place of periods, heighten our impression of someone in too big a hurry to take a pause, even in his thoughts. In *The Everlasting*, Leonard Bishop writes a two-page sex scene comprised of three very long sentences, which are actually short sentences conjoined by *and*. I'd quote from it, but my grandmother wouldn't approve.

Paragraphs

You probably remember from your English composition class that paragraphs are groups of sentences about the same idea. In *The Careful Writer*, Theodore Bernstein quotes Partridge as quoting Alexander Bain that "Between one paragraph and another there is a greater break in the subject than between one sentence and another."

Just as you will find your sentences have a natural rhythm as you write, so you will find that your paragraphs naturally fall into patterns of short, long and medium. Obviously, the content, tone and pace of your material will dictate this rhythm in part.

Longer paragraphs can make the same work seem denser, slower, but also more thoughtful. Very long paragraphs look more intimidating on the page, and a reader picking up a book for quick entertainment will not be thrilled to see them.

Short paragraphs can make a work seem faster paced, more simplistic, more accessible. Shorter paragraphs also create emphasis for their content. One-sentence paragraphs create the most emphasis of all.

Look at this paragraph:

When his three children lived with him it was always noisy at the table, with peas and insults flying. But the kids were living with Nancy. Now he ate alone.

Let's try it this way:

When his three children lived with him it was always noisy at the table, with peas and insults flying. But the kids were living with Nancy.
Now he ate alone.

The device of putting information into one-sentence paragraphs can be highly effective, but should not be overused. Pop writers sometimes rely on it too heavily as a way of making trite material seem more significant.

On another subject, remember that whenever a new person speaks, you must begin a new paragraph. You would *not* write:

"Where's my shawl?" Mrs. Potter asked. Her husband looked her up and down and then said dryly, "Where you left it, dear."

It would be correct to write:

"Where's my shawl?" Mrs. Potter asked.
Her husband looked her up and down then said dryly, "Where you left it, dear."

Although you can break the new-speaker, new-paragraph rule in the name of style, I'd suggest sticking to it, because otherwise you can cause confusion about who is speaking. When you confuse the reader you almost always lose more than you gain, because confusion merely frustrates the reader and reminds him he's reading a book. The way to get your point across is to lure the reader into your world and make him *forget* he's reading a book.

But while observing that rule, you still have options about where you break your paragraphs. In the above example, you might write:

"Where's my shawl?" Mrs. Potter asked. Her husband
looked her up and down then said dryly,
"Where you left it, dear."

A student of mine liked to break up many of his characters' short
speeches into paragraphs, for example:

"Ready, Henry?
"The meeting starts in an hour."

The new paragraph adds portent to the words, just as any new
paragraph will. However, no confusion is created because the omitted close quotes signify that the same person is speaking.

Scenes

We've been talking about scenes since chapter one. A scene is
continuous action, dramatized before our eyes. When the action
stops for an abrupt change in time or place, the scene ends. Scenes
are divided by so-called "space breaks" or "white spaces." That is,
you hit the return key an extra time. Sometimes writers put an
asterisk, or three asterisks, or some other cute little symbol, in that
white space (when I was ghostwriting a book about gender differences I alternated putting ♂s and ♀s in the space breaks).

Chunks of narration may be lumped with scenes, or they may
similarly be set apart with white spaces—depending, in part, on
how the narration relates to the scene. (If the narration describes
action that happens right before or after the scene it's more likely
to be part of the scene.)

You have a lot of options about scene breaks. You can make
them frequently, whenever there is a break in the time or place, or
you can write transitions that keep them going. Therefore, you can
manipulate scene breaks for the sake of the pace of your book, or
for emphasis. For example, let's say that you write a scene in which
children playing in a deserted field find a dead body. One of them
runs to get help. You can break the scene there and, after a white
space, tell us that you have returned to the same spot two hours
later where the other children are anxiously wondering what happened to little Timmy, and debate what their next move should
be. Or you can join the scenes together, by writing, "Two hours
later Timmy had not returned." Inserting the space break calls
attention to the lapse of time and makes it more ominous, but
maybe the scene is ominous enough without any further stress.

A transition such as "Two hours later," is pretty painless, and extremely useful, with or without a scene break. But scene breaks can help you skip those longer, and often needless, passages. For example, say your character is having a fight with his wife, and then has to rush to the airport to catch a plane. You can decide to follow a character from his house, into his car, and then to the airport. Or you can break the scene as he looks at his watch and begin the next scene as he's dashing down the jetway. The question is, do we need to see the man maneuver through traffic and hunt for a parking space at Midway? Maybe. Maybe he's going to observe an accident on the way and become a key witness. But if the point is merely to get him to the airport, then get him to the airport.

Short scenes create a faster-paced, but more disjointed book. Long scenes are more lifelike (after all, our lives are one long scene), but must be all the more dramatic, to keep the reader's interest.

Chapters

Someone asked me, not long ago, "How do you know when to break a chapter?"

Think of chapters as being to scenes as paragraphs are to sentences. Between chapters, there will be a greater break in the subject than there is between individual scenes.

Some novelists organize their chapters around another element of the book. For example, each chapter will be devoted to a different character's point of view, to a period of time (each chapter is a week or a month) or to a setting (each chapter is devoted to one of the countries on the heroine's European trip, or chapters alternate between two families in two different cities). But many novels won't lend themselves to these types of divisions—and even if yours can, you might choose not to put that constraint upon yourself.

When chapters don't break down naturally, and you don't want to squeeze them into a prearranged scheme, then you can look both at the growth of the characters and the movement of the plot in terms of how you do divide them. A longer lapse of time or a farther shift of distance than there is between other scenes might suggest new chapters. So, for example, with our man going to the airport, take-off might be a natural break, with the next chapter beginning with his arrival in Hong Kong. In a mystery, perhaps each chapter will provide a new clue, or discredit an old one.

Many of the early novels were serialized in monthly publications before being published as books. (This practice is rare but not unheard of today—Tom Wolfe's *Bonfire of the Vanities* was serialized in *The Village Voice* before it was published as a novel.) Because of this, novelists such as Dickens and Thackeray tried to end each installment with a good cliffhanger. However arbitrarily the convention of breaking up novels arose, it's a good thing. As David Lodge points out, "Breaking up a long text into smaller units . . . gives the narrative, and the reader, time to take a breath, as it were, in the intervening pauses."

Given this rule, such as it is, you can then be aware that authors can manipulate chapters, just as they manipulate scenes, for their own ends. Sue Grafton likes to flaunt the idea entirely by breaking her chapters mid-scene. However you break them, though, when you end a chapter, you give added emphasis to the end of the one and the beginning of the new.

Chapters can be grouped into parts, or sections, which are then numbered either with Roman numerals (I, II, III, IV) or the standard Arabic ones (1, 2, 3, 4). This is more common in longer novels. Or you can dispense with chapters and just divide the book into parts (this would work better in a short or medium-length novel; the parts would become like long chapters).

You don't need to divide a novel at all. Robert Stone's *A Flag for Sunrise* is divided neither into chapters nor parts, only scenes. It makes the novel more lifelike, but also denser and harder to follow.

At the other extreme, Joan Didion's *Play It as It Lays* is written in extremely short chapters, some of which are half a page. It adds to our experience of Maria Wyeth, the main character, as living a disjointed and aimless life.

Note that chapters don't have to be even of roughly equal length, although that's more common. Mixing long and short chapters can help us share the characters' changing experience of time. Shorter chapters can get us through less eventful periods, while a faster pace will hold our attention through longer chapters.

The Placement Principle

Sentences

The location of words within a sentence has an effect on how those words register in the reader's brain.

Consider these three sentences:

1. He was a thief, however.
2. However, he was a thief.
3. He was, however, a thief.

The word or phrase at the end of a sentence has the greatest impact on a reader, the beginning the second most, and the middle the least.

Paragraphs

The Placement Principle is equally true for sentences within paragraphs:

> I love to eat ice cream. They tell me it's fattening, but I don't care. I'm going to be eating ice cream on the day I die. Chocolate. That's my favorite. This morning the vendor with the cart on the corner tried to get me to buy Mocha Almond. Tomorrow I'm going to bring my .44 to the cart and blow his face off.

Look at the same paragraph rearranged:

> I love to eat ice cream. They tell me it's fattening, but I don't care. I'm going to be eating ice cream on the day I die. This morning the vendor with the cart on the corner tried to get me to buy Mocha Almond. Tomorrow I'm going to bring my .44 to the cart and blow his face off. Chocolate. That's my favorite.

The first version, with the threatening line at the end, is more menacing. Placing the threat to the ice cream vendor in the middle defuses it a little; we might even read it as a joke. Obviously, how we interpret this passage will depend on many factors having to do with the context as a whole, including what we already know about the speaker. But you can see how the placement of a key piece of information can affect our experience of it.

One of the things we can learn from the Placement Principle is that information buried in the middle of a paragraph can get overlooked. No matter how conscientious the reader, he doesn't want to feel as though he's studying for a test when he reads your novel. He's not going to memorize every line. An important event, such as a character's decision to leave his wife, deserves to be built up. If the final decision comes in the middle of a passage of reflection, we might miss it.

Scenes and Chapters

The Placement Principle also applies to scenes and chapters (and to chapters within the book itself). What comes at the end of a scene is the most memorable, what comes at the beginning the second most, what's imbedded in the middle the least. If the description of a particular room is important—say, it's going to function in the plot because the books on the shelves will provide a clue to the identity of the murderer—you might consider putting that at the beginning. If the description is less important—functioning primarily to let us see the action—it might belong in the middle.

Similarly, the scenes that begin and end a chapter will stay clearest in the reader's mind as he goes through the novel. And even in the book as a whole, although the novel should be full of vivid, dramatic scenes, you can bet that a few years after reading it, the beginning and end will be the most distinct parts in the reader's memory. (As an exercise, go to your bookshelf and pick out a couple of books you read more than two years ago and ask yourself—without looking at the book—what you most remember about it.) This is one of the several reasons that a strong beginning is so important, although it's not a reason to neglect the middle of the novel, in which the stakes should continually increase.

Literary writers sometimes use this principle to lend an artificial importance to trivial details, either in individual sentences, paragraphs or at the end of the story or novel itself. These are the kind of stories you used to see in the *New Yorker* (not as much anymore), in which the final image was something along the lines of, "A sparrow chirped," or "The kitchen was white." *Ooooh.*

When to Ignore the Placement Principle

You can see how the Placement Principle can help structure your novel into sentences, paragraphs, scenes and chapters. However, it would be burdensome, at best, to obsessively analyze each and every sentence as you write it with the Placement Principle in mind. As a rewriting tool, however, it can be enormously helpful. Sometimes it can even help you pinpoint why the flow of a manuscript is wrong. Like any rule in this book, if it gets in your way, forget about it.

Contemporary References

Brand names, references to famous people and current events can add authenticity to your work and help set it in time and place.

Often students ask me if it's legal to use brand names, like Coke or Pop Tarts. The answer is, Yes—it is. And it can be a helpful device as well. In terms of characterization, the kind of person who smokes Camels is different from the one who smokes Virginia Slims. And in terms of setting, just think of Bosco and Malt-o-Meal:

Don't they bring back the 1950s? Similarly, we associate Wells Fargo and Pinkerton men with the Old West, and names such as Oxydol, Texaco and Lucky Strikes with the old radio shows that they sponsored.

But don't let brand names substitute for the concrete and specific details that let the reader experience the action. For example, if you say that a woman is wearing Ferragamos, most readers will recognize this brand as an expensive, high-quality shoe. But that isn't the same as showing us a shiny patent leather pump, black as licorice—and we need those details as well. Brand names should be used to enhance the novel, by setting it in time and place and revealing the characters' personalities and backgrounds—not as a shorthand for the gritty facts themselves.

References to movie stars, politicians and current events can make the social milieu in which your characters live more vivid. How many of these references you include, though, depends upon your style and upon the content of the book itself.

Also remember that while in a certain kind of pop fiction, characters can board the Titanic, arrive in San Francisco in April of 1906 or invest their life savings in the stock market in the summer of 1929, in literary fiction an overabundance of these involvements in famous disasters will seem too convenient.

Titles

A title may seem a trivial consideration, but under most circumstances it's the name that your novel will bear throughout its life. (Very occasionally books are reissued under different titles, for example, to match the film that was made from the book but under a different name.)

There are two considerations in choosing a title for your book: one, the crass commercial, and the other the aesthetic.

Commercial Concerns

Let's deal with shallow commercial considerations first. In terms of selling your book, first to a publisher and then to the public, simple is good, and simple and catchy is better.

Two-word titles have always been popular, titles such as *Labor Pains, Continental Drift, Mixed Emotions, Hard Facts, Bare Bones, Customer Service, Time Out, Bad Breaks, Summer Magic, Sweet Talk, Pleasant Dreams, Life Force, Love Story*.

But slightly longer titles are common, too. *Queen of Hearts, Ace in the Hole, Man About Town, The Age of Innocence, A Is for Alibi*.

The catchiness of a title can derive from its literary sound. *How Green Was My Valley, Jacob Have I Loved, Ride a Cock Horse, After the Fall, Gone With the Wind*. Titles such as these sound as though they come from the Bible, Shakespeare, or from poetry—whether they do or not.

The catchiness can come from the jargon of the profession of the characters (and again, this would be a way of emphasizing what's important): *Back to You, Fred*, about a reporter, or *Car 54, Where Are You?* for the durable TV show about policemen in the Bronx. (In general, you can look to TV shows for catchy titles, if not impressive content.)

Currently, a popular trend in mystery fiction is to make some play of words on the idea of death or murder. *Rest in Pieces, But I Wouldn't Want to Die There, Caught Dead in Philadelphia, Death and Taxes*.

You want titles that are simple and catchy because that makes them easy to remember. And you want your title to be memorable because there's a lot of competition out there. Your book is probably one of the most important things in your life—possibly *the* most. It isn't to other people. If someone is standing in a bookstore, scratching his head and wondering, "Now let's see—was it *Hi Diddle Diddle* or *Fiddle-Dee-Dee?*" he will soon be distracted by the cover of another book. He will not necessarily ask for help in finding yours. Maybe he will—but why make it hard for him?

If that same buyer calls a store to ask for your book, it's of equal importance that he get the title right. Overly long, inventive titles pose the risk that this buyer will mix up a few words, and that the clerk punching the computer keys may mistakenly tell this potential buyer that the book isn't in stock. When your first book is published you will be calling up every bookstore in the three nearest area codes to make sure that everyone who works at each store is aware of it, but you won't be able to do that for every bookstore in the country.

A title should also indicate that your book is a work of fiction. Your novel will be one of hundreds shipped to the store that week. That same clerk, underpaid and overworked, sorting the books hurriedly, dreaming of his after-work date, isn't going to read the jacket copy on every volume. So you don't want to use a title that will put your novel on the wrong shelf. A title like *Ten Ways to Meet the Man of Your Dreams* might land you among the volumes on self-help.

Naturally, there are exceptions to these commercial considerations: In recent years Whitney Otto's *How to Make an American Quilt* and Nora Ephron's *Heartburn* were successful novels in spite of titles that could have gotten some people confused with the topics of home improvement or health. Lorrie Moore even published a book of short stories called *Self-Help*. There have also been long, potentially confusing titles that have graced the covers of best-sellers, like *Zen and the Art of Motorcycle Maintenance*.

But since even writers have to live in the real world, I think you should take these commercial considerations into account.

From a legal standpoint, you should know that titles aren't copy-rightable and many books have the same title. Sometimes these duplicate titles are even published within a few years of each other. The exception is that when a book becomes so well-known that using the same title could lead to confusion in the mind of the public, that title becomes pre-empted for future use. You can't call your novel *Catcher in the Rye* or, probably, *The Bible*.

The Aesthetic Factor

You can look upon your title as a final and not insignificant opportunity to direct the reader's attention to what you think is important in the novel. It's like the scarf you tie around your neck to bring out one of the colors of your ensemble. You can use your title to emphasize the setting, a key image or some aspect of the characters' lives or personalities.

David Lodge points out that, "The titles of the earliest English novels were invariably the names of the central characters, *Moll Flanders*, *Tom Jones*, *Clarissa*. Fiction was modeling itself on, and sometimes disguising itself as, biography and autobiography."

Today main character titles are less common. You might still choose one, perhaps to pay homage to the tradition of those early English novels, or to emphasize the importance of one of the main characters. (We discussed, in chapter two, the effect that the titles *Anna Karenina* and *The Great Gatsby* have of shifting the focus to those two characters.) Flaubert used the title *Madame Bovary*, which calls attention to Emma Bovary's married state. Since the book centers around her adulteries, this is significant; the title *Emma Bovary* would have had a different effect.

A character title can even provide a clue to the plot. *The Brothers Karamazov*, Dostoyevsky's masterpiece, may at first glance seem to refer to Ivan, Dmitri and Alyosha, the three men who share that last name. But there is another man who might also be their brother, who plays a pivotal role in the story, who is subtly included in that title, because of the word "brothers."

Titles that refer to a setting are fairly common, as in *Death in Venice*, *Wuthering Heights*, *Brideshead Revisited*, *California Street* and *Waverly Place*. Such a title should emphasize the importance of the setting in the novel. George Eliot's novel, *Middlemarch*, takes its title from the name of the town the many characters of her novel live in or near. It works well because the ambitions and the limitations of the characters are in some measure shaped by the fact that they come from a provincial town, and some of the plot deals with petty provincial politics.

Often an author will use a quote from another literary source as a title, although this is a less popular device than it once was. John Steinbeck wrote a book called *The Winter of Our Discontent*, a line from Shakespeare's *Richard III*. His novel, *The Grapes of Wrath* takes its title from "The Battle Hymn of the Republic." Hemingway's novel, *For Whom the Bell Tolls* takes its title from a poem by John Donne; another of his titles, *The Sun Also Rises*, comes from Ecclesiastes.

When you take a title from a previously published work of fiction, you evoke that work, calling attention to some influence of style or theme that that earlier work has on yours. This is the poem that gave Hemingway the title of *For Whom the Bell Tolls*:

No man is an *Iland*, intire of it selfe; every man is a peece of the *Continent*, a part of the *maine*; if *Clod* bee washed away the *Sea*, *Europe* is the lesse, as well as if a *Mannor* of thy *Friends* or of *thine owne* were; any mans *death* diminishes *me*, because I am involved in *Mankinde*; And therefore never send to know for who the *bell* tolls; It tolls for *thee*.

Hemingway's novel deals with a American who is fighting with the Republicans in the Spanish Civil War. In the end he dies to save the small band of guerrillas—or at least to give them more time. The title (reinforced by the poem which is used as an epigraph) allows Hemingway to underscore certain themes of the novel: the interconnectness of people and the tragedy of war. It also helps us understand how when Robert Jordan dies, we are all diminished.

Lorraine Hansberry used a quote from Langston Hughes's poem, "What Happens to a Dream Deferred?" for her play, *A Raisin in the Sun*, thus bringing to mind all of Hughes's memorable poem for her viewers.

REWRITING NOTES

Oakley Hall writes, "Perhaps the writers' true style begins to emerge when he makes no deliberate effort to produce one."

In that spirit, you may discover your style somewhat accidently-on-purpose as you reread your first draft. This is another example of how you as a writer are constantly balancing conscious and unconscious processes. Read that first draft as objectively as possible, as if you were an editor, and look for what stylistic patterns emerge: incomplete, staccato sentences, oblique dialogue, whimsical metaphors, or whatever. You can then take more conscious control over those patterns.

In my own work, at some point, I noticed a tendency to combine, sometimes in the same sentence, a more formal lanaguage with the vernacular. It wasn't something I set out to do originally, but once I saw that I was doing it, I purposely kept on doing it, gradually making it more my own.

However, you should also look at where those same stylistic patterns can become mannerisms that you may want to purge from your writing. I had a student who constantly tagged his characters' speech with one word descriptions of the emotions they were feeling:

> "Hi." Happy.
> "How are you?" Fearful.
> "Fine." More reserved now.

Since the tags were telling, not showing, the emotions, it was an ineffective device, and overuse made it downright annoying.

Although this example is pretty obvious, these patterns are sometimes difficult to see until you can read large chunks of your work at one sitting, after a short break from the work. Sometimes, too, the difference between style and a mannerism is overuse, or the appropriateness of the use.

Where you've imposed any artificial devices (like giving every character a first name that begins with the letter *J*), you have to ask yourself whether the device adds or detracts. Sometimes your answer will simply have to come from your gut—you can come up with a literary justification for anything. ("*J* is the first letter in the name Job, and the book is a homage to the Book of Job.")

Remember that personal style takes a long time to develop, and develops best in an unhurried fashion.

Additional Style Exercises:

1. Study a few pages of a stylish novel that you admire. Imitate that writer's style—very long or very short sentences, florid or spare prose—while writing about something completely different.

2. Write the most lurid sex scene you can imagine. You don't have to show it to anyone, but this exercise can help you confront lingering inhibitions about intimate material. As a variation, write about something completely different than your usual subject matter. For example, if you tend to write in a literary style, closely examining relationships, then write a heavy action scene, like a battle or a riot.

3. Rewrite a few pages of your own novel in a different tense. Include both scene and narration in the rewrite.

4. Create a new persona for yourself: a sixteenth-century pirate, a World War I army nurse, a famous movie star. Then write a scene as you imagine this person would write it. Remember, you are not writing as if this is a character who is your first-person narrator, you are writing as if *you* are this person, suddenly become a writer, to discover what his or her style is.

5. Go back to a plot outline you made of a novel (which you should have done after chapter three). Examine the scene breaks and chapter divisions.

6. Take a few pages of your novel that's primarily narration and change it to a passage that's primarily dialogue. Then take a passage of dialogue and change it to narration.

7. Make a list of twenty titles that you like.

CHAPTER SEVEN

Parting Words

At times I've feared that this book may seem a bit daunting, covering as it does so many aspects of craft. I'd like to make a final pitch to keep the spirit of play alive as you write. If you're going to do it, you might as well enjoy it.

On the last night of one of my classes, a student passed out copies of an inspirational piece she wrote and she generously gave me permission to quote from it here:

MISSION POSSIBLE: HOW TO WRITE A NOVEL

. . . Invent a glue that won't let you out of your chair for thirty-three pages. Or take long cuts. . . . Stay in bed the whole day. Dream of starry starry nights like Van Gogh. Don't follow the normal. Be absurd, be ridiculous. Find mosquitoes making love. Drink rainbows. Draw the hurts. Buy toys and put them in the bathtub. Wog with a child. Adopt a grandmother/grandfather.

Feel rich without money or Ferrari. Be who you truly are and the money will follow. Listen to the sounds of silence. Eat exotic fruits hanging upside down. Be proactive instead of reactive. Don't take critics seriously. . . .

. . . Play peace games. Wait for shooting stars. Watch for meteorites and comets. Play football. Be the quarterback of your manuscript. Expect to be sacked, bloodied, injured, intercepted, and tackled on your way to the goal line. When it's fourth down, take a risk and go for it. . . .

Drink twenty-five cups of tea in one sitting like Dr. Samuel Johnson. Then you'll have to go to the bathroom. A reminder to get rid of garbage language. Revise. Rewrite.

Rewrite. Rewrite. Rewrite until your hands can no longer
type or write.

—Elizabeth Nisperos

In other words, work hard and have some fun at the same time.

One of the most marvelous things about writing is that nothing
in your life is wasted. As a writer, you have all the more reason to
go out and do a variety of things. If you go hang-gliding, you'll be
able to use it in your work. Maybe you'll write a scene about hang-
gliding, or maybe you'll graft the feelings of fear and exhilaration
you experience onto a different episode in a character's life.

If you must work a day job, as many writers do, then that can
be material, too. A student of mine, returning to work as a financial
consultant after a year spent writing, told me, "I've decided to be
successful at two careers." He had the right attitude. Sure, it's unfair
that we live in a society that doesn't support all of us who want to
write in the lifestyle to which we aspire. But since most of us don't
have the luxury of that lifestyle anyhow, there's no reason not to
make the best of it. Being good at teaching, nursing or building
houses will make you a better writer, not a worse one.

So enjoy life and enjoy your other career if you have one. Enjoy
your family and friends. The only limitation is that you must make
sure you leave yourself time to write, too.

A final thought about technique: I don't believe in knee-jerk
criticism. No, I don't like flashbacks, but sometimes they work. I
think a novel needs a strong plot, but the type of plot that suffices
for an individual novel will vary.

When you look at your own work, as well as when you look at
the work of others, look at it as a whole, and try to judge it on its
own terms. You can't just check off a number of requirements and,
if the manuscript fulfills them, consider it finished.

Appraising your own work, of course, is a tough job. It's often
tempting to circumvent doing another draft or simply avoid the
hard truth that something isn't working. On the other hand, you
also need to recognize the point at which you've taken a novel as
far as you can.

Above all, keep writing. I will be picturing you, bending over
your notepads and keyboards, in cafés and at bus stops, at your
desk when your boss isn't looking, and at the kitchen table after
everyone goes to bed.

INDEX